NICK POE

LOUDER

A DEVOTIONAL THAT'S NOT ABOUT YOU

WESTBOW
PRESS®
A DIVISION OF THOMAS NELSON
& ZONDERVAN

WestBow Press books may be ordered through booksellers or by contacting:

WestBow Press
A Division of Thomas Nelson & Zondervan
1663 Liberty Drive
Bloomington, IN 47403
www.westbowpress.com
1 (866) 928-1240

ISBN: 978-1-5127-4572-6 (sc)
ISBN: 978-1-5127-4573-3 (hc)
ISBN: 978-1-5127-4571-9 (e)

Library of Congress Control Number: 2016909632

Print information available on the last page.

WestBow Press rev. date: 06/13/2016

CONTENTS

I dedicate this book to my parents Brian and Charlotte Poe. You always said 'yes' to the things that would better me, and you only said 'no' to the things that would hurt me. I love you.

INTRODUCTION

This is a devotional that is not about you. It's about those you will encounter today. It's about the people who need what you have to give. If your personal devotion doesn't produce a public influence, it isn't getting the job done.

As I recently spoke with a certain pastor, I was told that in his particular denomination, the word "evangelism" had become a dirty word. Many folks are a-okay with you being a Christian—they just don't want you talking about it. The goal of the devil is to muzzle the church, causing her to grow quieter and quieter, eventually rendering her silent. That's a problem in light of the truth that we are called to be *loud*. Christianity has never been a private affair. It's always been a public confession. Satan wants to strip us of our ability to give Jesus to somebody who doesn't have Him.

I write this devotional with the intention of exhorting believers daily to never lose their voice. Your platform for influence is found in your home, your workplace, and your marketplace. If our only pulpit is within the walls of a church, we have grown secluded and ineffective. Jesus meant it when He said to go into "all the world."

Within these pages, you will find instruction for influence, along with many authentic stories—from my life as well as the lives of others. The Bible is sure to give information as well as inspiration, and any book should do the same. Together, let's build bridges of irresistible influence. The world has a message to preach. The church has a better one. Will you be louder?

Something Real

> If one of you says to them, "Go in peace; keep warm and well fed," but does nothing about their physical needs, what good is it? (James 2:16 NIV)

The world is grasping for authenticity. Society feeds on fiction and consequently lives with a truth deficit. People you see every day are in search of answers. Real answers. Hypocrisy displayed in the church has caused people to see the house of God not as a place for an answer, but as part of the problem. You and I, living in genuine devotion to Jesus, have the ability to renovate the image of the church. The folks you encounter from day to day should never again be able to say that all Christians are hypocrites—because they met you. You're the exception. A "Christian" confession isn't worth much in our culture; however, a Christian lifestyle changes the culture.

I know a man who was working a desk job at a hotel in our city. As his shift ended, he noticed a homeless couple come into the lobby to warm up before moving on. Being moved with compassion, he approached them and said, "My shift ends in a few minutes, so stick around for a bit … I have something for you." After clocking out, he invited the couple in, gave them a significant amount of money and said, "I want you to know, the only reason I'm doing this for you is because Jesus is my Lord." The homeless man began crying and hugged him. He proceeded by telling the couple, "There is a condition with the money I gave you. Half of it is for you. Do with it as you please. But the other half I want you to give away to someone else in need, because I want you to see that the joy isn't just in receiving, but it's in the giving."

The couple agreed humbly. That night, both folks got right with God and committed themselves to Jesus. As the weeks passed by, the couple reconnected with the man, and the testimonies poured in about how the other half of the money was used. The couple divided it up and began paying for meals for local people. The poorest people in the community went about blessing others financially. God has a way of pouring Himself into the most unlikely vessels.

If we reduce influence to the church pulpit, these sorts of testimonies become extinct. Hypothetically, if the early apostles would have limited church to a building, the book of Acts would not be 28 chapters. In fact, it would have been about one chapter—detailing the end of the church and nothing more. As you navigate through life, display something real to humanity. Find opportunity to give away a genuine gospel that the world can sink its teeth into. The capacity to change the world is in you.

Today, will you exercise your world changing influence?

Father, You haven't just called me to preach a message but to display a person. Let the genuineness of Christ be all over my life. I'm not trying to sell something or put up a façade. I'm giving away something real. Thank You for empowering me for this work! I pray this in Jesus' name, amen.

Flowing

> Whoever believes in me, as Scripture has said, rivers of living water will flow from within them. (John 7:38 NIV)

A river flows from a source that's bigger than itself, and it flows into a body bigger than itself. Your ministry source is a God who is bigger than you. Your ministry target is a hurting humanity that's bigger than you. You're the conduit through which God wants to nourish the earth.

Jesus came to save the world. A lot of the world hasn't found out about it because a lot of the church hasn't talked about it. There is no substitution for Christ-like influence. It's time to vote silence off the island—it never did anything for you anyway.

You can't accept Jesus for the world, but you can live a life that makes it a whole lot easier for the world to say yes. In the workplace, a Christian witness is dissolved by lousy work ethic. Your testimony can be hampered by a complaining attitude. Our gospel is most clearly communicated when backed by a life that shows the evidence of it. A voiceless church is a dying church. We must not build a sanctuary for our timidity or protect our fear of speaking out. If we really believe that Jesus is the best thing to ever hit the planet, we will have no problem advertising Him boldly with our lives.

The book of Acts quotes Jesus saying, "It is more blessed to give than to receive" (Acts 20:35 NIV). It's very simple: giving is a superior blessing than receiving. Many search for blessing by spending their lives and energy on receiving from God, when receiving actually offers an inferior blessing. Dwell in the superior. Absorbing what you can is good. Giving what you have is even better.

Today, will you offer the very life that's been offered to you?

Father, my desire is to give. May charity be found in my DNA. Lord, let us never receive from You only to hoard it for ourselves. Everything we have is to be poured out. Thank You for empowering us for this very thing, dear Father. In Jesus' name I pray, amen.

DAY 3

Seeds

> While the earth remains, Seedtime and harvest, Cold and heat, Winter and summer, And day and night Shall not cease. (Genesis 8:22 NASB)

The principle of sowing and reaping is riddled throughout the Bible. It's well understood that we reap what we sow, but we must also understand that we reap more than what we sow. An oak tree is much bigger than an acorn, thus the harvest is bigger than the initial seed.

In the realm of personal evangelism, the simple seed of the gospel is planted within individuals so that a harvest will be brought in the form of a life eternally remaining in the presence of God. Praying for an end time harvest of souls without ever planting the Word in lives around you is like expecting crops to grow in a field that no one has touched.

Jesus said the kingdom of God is "as if a man should scatter seed on the ground" (Mark 4:26 ESV). The ground is fertile in your workplace. It's fertile in your family. It's fertile in the marketplace.

Take a coworker to lunch. Pick up the bill for the person behind you at the coffee shop. Pray for a stranger in the grocery store. Leave a generous tip paired with a note of encouragement for your waitress. I believe that it's easier to radically bless people than we might think.

Today, will you be the person who scatters seed—or will you withhold it?

Father, I thank You that You have given seed to the sower. May You use me this day to spread the seed of Your Word throughout humanity. Give me opportunity to pray for the sick, share with the needy, and plant the gospel in the hearts of the lost. I trust that the seed I sow today will reap an eternal harvest to the glory of God. In Jesus' name, amen.

Repairing the Breach

Those from among you Shall build the old waste places; You shall raise up the foundations of many generations; And you shall be called the Repairer of the Breach, The Restorer of Streets to Dwell In. (Isaiah 58:12 NKJV)

Reconciliation creates a bridge for healthy influence. During my senior year of high school, I experienced a radical one eighty in which in a short time I went from seeking the lust of the flesh to seeking the living God. I remember approaching a girl who I was rude to as a sinner and apologizing, telling her that I had my life straight now. She didn't believe me, assuming that I was being sarcastic. When that sort of a transition happens, sometimes people need to see the Jesus you live before they believe the Jesus you preach. Eventually, she saw the change and knew that I was a transformed young man.

Months later, we were caught up in a sort of spiritual conversation. She seemed nonchalant in her tone, but I could sense that she was seeking answers. She needed help. We separated from the group of people around us, and I was able to sit with her for a time of counseling and prayer. She told me that at night, her mother would wake up screaming, "Get away from me, get away from me!" This girl would hear voices. In fact, she would hear her name called. Additionally, she felt she was being spit on by unseen forces.

When she told me this, I knew it was demonic in origin. I began to tell her the source of these attacks—demons. The girl was so afraid and tormented that she would sleep on the couch at night. I don't remember the last time she said she had a good night's rest. At the conclusion of our counseling, I laid my hand upon her head and prayed. I don't remember what I prayed exactly. But I can remember using the blood of Jesus and the name of Jesus. Those weapons may be simple, but you had better believe that they are absolutely pristine.

We departed, and throughout the day and that night after arriving home, I prayed earnestly that the Lord would give her rest that night. The next morning, I sat down in class. She approached me and without saying anything hugged me. I asked, "How did you sleep last night?" And she said, "I slept so well; I didn't even get up for school on time." For the first time in a long while, she received rest. Jesus has compassion that never sits still. He reaches so far into the struggles of humanity and gladly performs the miraculous.

The reason that I was positioned to minister the love and power of Jesus to this young lady was because I first went to her and apologized for my previous actions. I made things right and conveyed my new life to her. If your friends, colleagues, and family still see you as the person you used to be, your ministry to them may lack credibility. It's important that you bridge the gap with those around you and express the newness of life that you now walk in.

Today, is there anyone whom you could not witness to successfully because of a broken bridge? Could you make things right, and position yourself to be a life giving source in the life of that person?

Father, I thank You that my salvation is not a secret. I desire to show every person I encounter that I am no longer who I used to be. I am a minister of the gospel of Jesus Christ. Lord, position me to pray for those who are bound and watch as You break the bonds of the evil one through the blood of Your Son Jesus. I pray this in Jesus' name, amen.

An Uncontainable Message

> For we cannot but speak the things which we have seen
> and heard. (Acts 4:20 NKJV)

In the first chapter of Jeremiah, God called Jeremiah at the young age of 17 to be a messenger of the Lord. Reluctant to accept this great calling, Jeremiah said, "Ah, Lord God! Behold, I cannot speak, for I am only a youth" (Jeremiah 1:6NKJV). The young man made an excuse as to why he wasn't qualified for the job. God doesn't want an excuse. God wants a yes.

Eventually, Jeremiah accepted this call and went on to become one of the most renowned prophets in the history of Israel. In Jeremiah 20:9NKJV, he uttered these famous words: "But His word was in my heart like a burning fire Shut up in my bones; I was weary of holding it back, And I could not." Think with me: in Jeremiah chapter 1, he said, "I cannot speak," but by Jeremiah chapter 20, he said, "I cannot hold it in." I believe this is a picture of what God wants to do in the heart of His church. He wants to make the fearful as bold as the lion, because a timid preacher is an ineffective preacher.

I've heard Christians talking about being afraid to witness to strangers. God wills to destroy this mentality so that Christians aren't hesitant of witnessing; rather they are hesitant of keeping silent.

Today, do you believe that you have a word from God inside of you that cannot be contained? Make it a point to live with one singular option—sharing this Jesus whom you have seen and heard.

Father, I thank You that Your word is like a fire within me. Help me to spread the fire of Your word and Spirit to the world that is before me. I declare that I cannot and will not suppress the evangelistic desire that is within me. Lord, I am Your change agent in the earth. Use me this day. I pray in Jesus' name, amen!

DAY 6

Let Me Bring a Crowd With Me

> But you be watchful in all things, endure afflictions, do the work of an evangelist, fulfill your ministry. (2 Timothy 4:5 NKJV)

Shortly after their own personal salvation, many Christians surge with evangelistic desire. They'll share the news with family, knock on doors, hand out tracts, and pray for the sick. Sadly for many, this fire is doused with religion, fear, and the cares of this life. God doesn't intend on this fire being put out; rather He wants it kindled continually.

Less than 2 months after being saved, I wrote a prayer in my Bible: "Lord, someday I'll see You in heaven, and when I do—let me bring a crowd with me." I began to witness on the streets and in my school, as well. Other seasoned Christians would comment, "You are really on fire for God, aren't you?" This didn't sit well with me because it seemed to imply that being "on fire for God" was a seasonal occurrence. I wasn't on fire for the time being, I was on fire in an inextinguishable way.

I want to challenge you, if you're on fire for Jesus—stay on fire. If you're not on fire for Jesus—get on fire and keep the fire. Fuel the flame with the divine duo of Word and Spirit. Many can't recall the last time they talked about Jesus with someone outside of the church. The crowd of 120 in the upper room would have grown no larger than 120 if they would have stayed in the room. The key to the expansion of their group was the fact that they hit the streets of Jerusalem, ready to minister power to the lost.

Today, will you hit the streets of your personal Jerusalem willing and ready to point the world to our King?

Father, I thank You for placing within me a desire for personal evangelism. I want to touch the lost, encourage the church, and set on fire the lukewarm. Someday I'll see You in heaven, and when I do—let me bring a crowd with me. In Jesus' name, amen.

Endued with Power

> And being assembled together with them, He commanded them not to depart from Jerusalem, but to wait for the Promise of the Father, "which," He said, "you have heard from Me; for John truly baptized with water, but you shall be baptized with the Holy Spirit not many days from now. (Acts 1:4–5 NKJV)

It's post-resurrection and pre-ascension in the earthly life of Christ. Jesus gathers His apostles and shares specific direction, leading to the Holy Ghost kick start of the early church.

Notice that Jesus commands the apostles not to depart from Jerusalem until the coming of the Holy Spirit. Why? Because they could not carry out the work that God had for them until they were first filled with the Holy Spirit. Although they knew Jesus, had a relationship with Him, and were familiar with the gospel, if they would have dispersed and left Jerusalem without the baptism of the Holy Ghost—the apostles would have been ill equipped for the task at hand. It is the will of God for all believers to be filled with the Spirit (see Ephesians 5:18). The Holy Ghost doesn't have an expiration date.

"When the Day of Pentecost had fully come, they were all with one accord in one place. And suddenly there came a sound from heaven, as of a rushing mighty wind, and it filled the whole house where they were sitting. Then there appeared to them divided tongues, as of fire, and one sat upon each of them. And they were all filled with the Holy Spirit and began to speak with other tongues, as the Spirit gave them utterance" (Acts 2:1–4 NKJV).

Jump to verse 11 and the text describes the tongues which they spoke: "Cretans and Arabs—we hear them speaking in our own tongues the wonderful works of God."

In verse 2, Holy Spirit fills "the whole house," yet He isn't just interested in filling the house—He is interested in filling the people. Notice, when Holy Spirit fills the house, it's the sound of a rushing mighty wind. When Holy Spirit fills man, it's the sound of tongues declaring the works of God. Consider it: the Holy Spirit fills the house and it's the sound of wind, but it's not until He fills man that the sound is the works of God being declared! God wants to use you to declare His works. The Spirit of God could have showed up and declared the wonderful works on His own, but He chose to use our voice.

An evangelist once told me, "Teaching on evangelism without teaching the baptism of the Holy Ghost is like spitting in the wind."

Today, be filled with the Holy Ghost, for your power to witness comes not from Bible reading or theological knowledge. It comes from the Holy Spirit resting upon you (see Acts 1:8).

Father, I thank You for filling me with Your precious Spirit. By faith, I stir myself up by praying in the Holy Spirit, trusting that You are empowering me and gracing me to be Your chosen witness. May You grant to me more than my heart can hold—that I would live in a constant state of overflow. I pray these things in the name of Jesus, amen.

Moving in Power

And they went out and preached everywhere, the Lord working with them and confirming the word through the accompanying signs. Amen. (Mark 16:20 NKJV)

Signs and wonders aren't a bonus to evangelistic ministry—they're a requirement. If I share Jesus with someone lost and dying of a terminal disease, I must share Jesus the Savior as well as Jesus the Healer. Shortly after coming to Jesus, I had seen footage of folks ministering in power on the streets, operating in the gifts of the Spirit and watching God heal. I liked the idea of authentic Christianity.

As I set out to move in God's power on the street for the very first time, I struck up conversation with a local man. I heard myself ask him about back pain. By the Holy Ghost, I identified the specific location of the pain and what was causing it. With his permission, I laid hands on him in prayer, and afterward he said that the pain was gone. I was getting my feet wet in Holy Ghost inspired evangelism. I didn't have to earn the gifts of the Spirit. I just yielded to the gifts of the Spirit. God didn't use me because I had great experience—I had none. He used me because I had willingness.

Paul said, "Pursue love, and desire spiritual gifts, but especially that you may prophesy." (1 Corinthians 14:1 NKJV) Why desire spiritual gifts? Because when we desire spiritual gifts, it positions us to be used in those gifts. The gifts of Spirit put an indisputable divine touch to your witness, which you cannot go without.

Today, will you ask the Holy Spirit to move through you in such gifts? Will you step out in humble availability for Jesus to do what He does best through you?

Father, I thank You that my ministering is not in word only but in demonstration of the Spirit's power. Your Kingdom is not a matter of talk, but power. Back up the word I share with signs, wonders, and miracles. I'm not satisfied with a power shortage in my life and ministry. Help me demonstrate this power of the gospel—spirit, soul, and body. I pray this in Jesus' name, amen.

So Loving the World

For God so loved the world … (John 3:16 NKJV)

If you attempt to change the world without loving the world, you will depart from godly influence and move over into manipulation. The lost will believe that God so loved the world when they see the church so love the world.

"Do you not know that the unrighteous will not inherit the kingdom of God? Do not be deceived. Neither fornicators, nor idolaters, nor adulterers, nor homosexuals, nor sodomites, nor thieves, nor covetous, nor drunkards, nor revilers, nor extortioners will inherit the kingdom of God" (1 Corinthians 6:9–10 NKJV).

No doubt, Paul lays out a straightforward list. But I want you to notice what he says in the very next verse: "And such were some of you …"

Paul doesn't remind them of their past to lay chains of regret and condemnation on them. Instead, when we remember where we've been, it reminds us to have compassion on those who are still there. If we're not careful, we will look at sinners in disgust, despising them—as if we didn't used to be one. Don't expect the morality of a Christian to be displayed in a sinner. If you don't have love, you don't have a ministry and you don't have a voice. What you have is a sounding brass or a clanging cymbal.

Today, if you haven't already—fall in love with the people of the world. Love is the track that a godly influencer should ride on.

Father, I thank You that I am compelled by love solely and completely. Unless I minister with Your authentic love, I am ministering in vain. Cause love to flood my being for this lost and dying generation. Your agape love is my desire, and I shall give it away. In Jesus' name, amen.

The Reason

> Each of you should give what you have decided in your heart to give, not reluctantly or under compulsion, for God loves a cheerful giver. (2 Corinthians 9:7 NIV)

Ministering out of religious obligation steals the joy of ministry right from you. Sharing Jesus should be a desire rather than a duty. Proclaiming the gospel isn't presenting a sales pitch. A salesman is in it for himself. A gospel preacher is in it for the sake of the world.

It's a mistake to reach out to someone if you're inspired by a guilty impulse to reach out. You shouldn't pray for the sick because you'd feel condemned if you didn't. You pray for the sick because you're in love with people and the God who created them. It's vital that we say what we say and do what we do because we are compelled by love. If we are driven by anything but love, we have the wrong fuel in our tank. Putting diesel fuel in a gasoline engine will result in serious problems. The machinery won't function properly. Running a Christian on religious motives will produce a lackluster outcome.

Today, don't allow the responsibility of personal evangelism to suck the life out of you. Let it inject life into you! What you do isn't as important as why you do it. Come before God and let your motives be pure, keeping yourself in the love of God and the patience of Christ (see 2 Thessalonians 3:5).

Father, I thank You that my motives are one hundred percent pure in Your sight. I will go forth today with a pure heart, dispensing what I have to a world that I love. I refuse to minister out of a religious obligation or guilty compulsion. My life and ministry are condemnation free zones. I have one reason that I minister—love. I pray this in Jesus' name, amen.

DAY 11

Sealing the Deal

...if you confess with your mouth the Lord Jesus and believe in your heart that God has raised Him from the dead, you will be saved. (Romans 10:9 NKJV)

We generally call this the prayer of salvation. We might more accurately call it the confession of salvation. While ministry has many goals, the salvation of souls must be top priority. Whether it's a public altar call or a personal invitation, we yearn to watch Romans 10:9 fleshed out among humanity.

The first person I ever personally led to Jesus was a girl I went to high school with. I informed her of the free gift of salvation and eternal life. She repeated a prayer after me to be saved. It seemed as though she was just going through the motions and the prayer did nothing internally—it was a very unspiritual and casual moment.

She told me months later that the after praying that prayer with me, she went to sleep that night—only to be awakened by what she described as her heart being "on fire." She knew it was Him. She dove into God's Word, grew, connected herself to a church, and is still happily serving the Lord to this day. If I were to take the initial salvation at face value, I might become discouraged, thinking that the prayer didn't stick. Don't discount what God has done simply because you don't see a sensational manifestation or immediate change. The Holy Spirit is in the business of following up with people.

Today, don't underestimate what your prayers and words are doing behind the scenes in the lives around you. For we walk by faith, not by sight (2 Corinthians 5:7 NASB).

Father, I thank You that people are touched by this gospel in bigger ways than I might see initially. I trust that You will bring me into situations in which I can extend an invitation to believe and confess Jesus to those who don't know Him. Thank You for following up with the people we touch by bringing them into unforgettable encounters. In Jesus' name, amen.

DAY 12

Stepping Into Your Uncomfortable Zone

> Have I not commanded you? Be strong and courageous.
> Do not be frightened, and do not be dismayed, for the Lord
> your God is with you wherever you go. (Joshua 1:9 NKJV)

The phrase "comfortable Christianity" is often an oxymoron. The gospel demands acts, ways, and lifestyle out of us that can't be accomplished within the borders of a comfort zone. In fact, a comfort zone is better defined as a non-influential box that the devil would like to keep you in. The Scriptures are full of men and women who didn't protect their comfort zone, but instead dismantled them.

It's not always comfortable to forget the opinion of the crowd. It's not always comfortable to pray for a stranger or give Jesus to someone who might reject you ... then again, it's even more uncomfortable to watch people die in sin.

When we protect our traditions and comfort zones, usually we're protecting strongholds that God wants to break down. Jesus stated it's possible to, "make the word of God of no effect *through your tradition*" (Mark 7:13 NKJV emphasis added). Tradition is comfortable. Reformation isn't. When I wanted to step out of my comfort zone, I got around people who had stepped out of theirs. We could go with the flow and look like the world, or we could swim against the tide and look like Jesus. Let's pick.

Today, will you swim against the tide of culture that Jesus would be exalted? Together, I believe we can change the direction of the current.

Father, I place my comfort zone on the altar before You. I no longer will stay bound by the limitations of my own personal comfort. Holy Spirit, help me to step up and step out with love in my heart and a bold message on my lips. In Jesus' name, amen.

Knowing the Source

> For we do not wrestle against flesh and blood, but against principalities, against powers, against the rulers of the darkness of this age, against spiritual hosts of wickedness in the heavenly places. (Ephesians 6:12 NKJV)

On the cover of *USA Today* on May 16, 2013, I noticed an article titled, "Why the military hasn't stopped sexual abuse." While theories and ideas may abound, the answer is quite biblically clear. The military hasn't stopped sexual abuse because the military hasn't stopped the devil. This abuse (or any other for that matter) isn't a flesh and blood sort of battle; instead, it's a battle with the spirit behind it all. People all over the world are losing the fight because they have failed to distinguish who their enemy is.

Jesus prayed, "Your kingdom come. Your will be done on earth as it is in heaven" (Matthew 6:10 NKJV). We yearn to see heaven on earth; however, if we want to see heaven on earth, we must first confront the agony on earth. If you don't recognize that you're in a battle, then you're already losing.

Your sphere of influence is also a battle ground. I once heard pastor Virginia Maasbach say, "The best spiritual warfare is holy living."

Today, I encourage you to discern your battle. In ministering to the depressed and oppressed, target the source of the symptoms in your prayer. Medicating darkness won't get rid of the darkness; turning on the light does that.

Father, I thank You that today I wage good warfare as a soldier of Christ. In dealing with Your people today, help me to see the bigger picture of the battle. I won't live as though there is a devil under every rock, but I will understand that I am in warfare with very real unseen forces. I will exercise my delegated authority this day and watch the world around me be influenced the One who is inside of me. In Jesus' name, amen.

Illogical Influence

> You come to me with a sword, with a spear, and with a javelin. But I come to you in the name of the Lord of hosts, the God of the armies of Israel, whom you have defied. (1 Samuel 17:45 NKJV)

Imagine yourself overlooking a field. On one end, you see the army of Israel. As you scan across to the other side of the field, you see a giant man named Goliath who needs to be taken down. As far as you can see, physically speaking, the army has everything needed to bring down the giant (swords, shields, and armor) —yet they can't do it.

Along comes a ruddy teenage shepherd boy named David. As far as you can see, physically speaking, he does not have any essentials for bringing down the giant (no sword, shield, or armor) —yet he slays the Philistine!

What's the difference? The army was equipped with what they needed naturally; David was equipped with what he needed spiritually. Because the army was ill equipped spiritually, it kept them from operating in what they had naturally. Because they weren't properly aligned with heaven, the fear of man kept them out of action, whereas David knew his God and this propelled him into action. This act defied logic in an extraordinary way. We often crave natural, logical explanations when Jesus said we'd be led into truth. Truth supersedes logic.

The extreme capacity for influence that is on your life as a believer is illogical. It doesn't make sense that such ordinary people could accomplish such miraculous exploits.

Today, be a giant killer. You may look small standing next to the giant, but the giant looks microscopic standing next to your God.

Father, I know that You have what it takes to get the job done. Knowing that I am spiritually equipped with every good thing, I will run to the giant and conquer. Let such victories bring about genuine revival in my family, in my workplace, and in my city. In Jesus' name I pray, amen.

Evangelizing the Church

> Therefore, as we have opportunity, let us do good to all
> people, especially to those who belong to the family of
> believers. (Galatians 6:10 NIV)

Outreach minded people must learn to navigate their calling
in such a way that they don't pursue the lost with an excessive
fixation that causes them to neglect those who are already saved.
Let us pursue the lost while cherishing the church. The Scripture
says "do good to all" with a special emphasis on "the family of
believers." If we set out to influence the lost only, we are losing half
of the battle. Christians everywhere have need of godly influence,
encouragement, healing, and support.

Ministers all over the planet live with chronic frustration. Pastors
all over the world are notorious for stress. Many believers carry
more frustration than nonbelievers and this should not be. God
wants to alleviate such burdens and show us how to walk with the
easy yoke and light burden described by Jesus.

Let us not only evangelize the lost but evangelize the church also. To evangelize means to "preach the gospel." Your fellow brothers and sisters in the Lord are in dire need of the refreshing Good News message that saved them to begin with.

Today, as a Christian, aim to reach the lost, thus adding to the Body, while never neglecting to love your brethren, thus edifying the Body.

Father, whether they're lost or found, people are the target of my love and devotion. I make it my aim to remember the church. Lord, bring hurting and broken believers into my life that they may receive edification and refreshing. If I have anything to do with it, Your Bride won't be neglected but she will be perfected. I pray all of this in the wonderful name of Jesus Christ, amen.

Balanced Ministry

> But I fear, lest somehow, as the serpent deceived Eve by his craftiness, so your minds may be corrupted from the simplicity that is in Christ. (2 Corinthians 11:3 NKJV)

When we strain out secondary items and side projects, Christianity is boiled down to a very simple life: loving God and loving people. Our commission is pointing the world to the total plan of redemption through Christ's love demonstrated at the cross. If we have a misdirected focus, our ministering can become goofy and strange—having an appearance of spirituality but lacking power. It's important that we don't make secondary items primary and make primary items secondary.

For example, I once ministered on the street with a few guys I got connected with locally. I watched as one of the guys prayed for a couple of girls on the street. He didn't stand in the gap for them and believe God for transformation, peace, and reconciliation. Instead, he laid hands on them and asked God to give them a sensation, warmth, or some sort of a physical feeling. He asked, "Do you feel anything?" They didn't seem to take the prayer seriously and replied, "No." The man seemed surprised and looked at other guys in the group as if wondering, why didn't it work?

This sort of ministering never sat well with me. I am 100 percent for manifestations of God's power and physical touch—in fact, I long for God to move in such ways to demonstrate His awesome presence. I've lain on the floor of a number of churches under His remarkable weight of glory. However, my goal isn't a physical manifestation. My goal is for hearts to lean in the direction of Jesus. If people feel things physically—fantastic! But it certainly isn't the biblical focus of our preaching. If someone gets goosebumps when I pray but walks away unchanged —I'm unsatisfied.

Today, as you set out to minister, keep the simplicity of Christ Jesus in the forefront of your thinking. We are directing mankind to the simple cross of Calvary. Pray for the Lord to stretch forth His hand and touch people with signs and wonders; however, don't live from one manifestation to the next. Remember, we walk by faith and not by sight, feeling, or sensation.

Father, I pray that You would use me in the miraculous. I want Your people touched in powerful ways through the sharing of this gospel and through the prayer of faith. Whether we feel anything or not, we know that You're responding. Help us to keep a healthy balance in the ministry You've set before us. In Jesus' name, amen.

Don't Wait

> And do this, knowing the time, that now it is high time to awake out of sleep; for now our salvation is nearer than when we first believed. (Romans 13:11 NKJV)

Heaven won't present you with the opportunity to lead a sinner to Jesus. Sinners won't be there. Evangelism to the lost is unique to this earth and this time. We pass by people every day that will die in their sin if we don't open our mouth. Procrastination isn't a bad habit. It is disobedience. I once heard someone say "delayed obedience is disobedience." In terms of proclaiming the gospel, there has never been a better time than now. There has never been a better day than today.

I met a man once who had lived a life of rebellion and disobedience to the Lord. He was diagnosed with a horrendous case of cancer. In dire straits, he got born again and gave his life over to the Lord Jesus. As he was in the hospital, he was watching christian television. A nurse walked in and asked if he was a Christian. He explained his recent conversion. Then he asked, "What about you?" The nurse was unsaved. At that moment, he gave Jesus to the nurse and she got born again. He described it as "the greatest blessing of his life." He was dead the next morning.

Don't wait until your days are almost over to be a bold witness of God. I'm sure if that man could go back, he would have started sooner. Evangelism is for today, because tomorrow might not be available. That is not a gloom and doom statement of unbelief—it's a statement of reality.

Father, thank You that You are satisfying me with long life, and in that long life I will make effort daily to bring many into Your perfect covenant of grace through Jesus Christ. Help me to not delay, for now is the time and today is the day of salvation. In Jesus' name, amen.

An Injection of Urgency

...Surely I am coming quickly. (Revelation 22:20 NKJV)

God chose to close out His Word in an interesting way. Three times in the last chapter of the Bible, Jesus declared the phrase, "I am coming quickly." He did not say, "I'm taking my time." The Lord injected a serious sense of urgency into the final passages of the Scriptures.

There is no such thing as an apathetic soul winner. Jesus won't tarry forever. We must be moved with godly urgency and love to reach further and go deeper. You and I should be in somewhat of a hurry to see to it that the job gets done. Don't wait to be qualified for a task you've already been ordained to carry out. Thirsty souls seek living water. Will you be a wellspring of life for the folks you encounter every day?

I personally know a wonderful pastor who would hang out at a park consistently with various people in his city. There was one young man in particular whom he felt he should minister the gospel to. The Holy Spirit would consistently urge him to share;

yet he didn't. He suppressed the leading because he wanted to build better relationship with the young man before introducing the gospel. A short time later, the young man died, unsaved, in a car accident. At the funeral, a friend of the man approached the pastor and said, "He kept talking about you before he passed and always wanted to know what was different about you." The pastor kept the obituary on his office desk for some time as a sobering reminder to quickly yield to unction to witness. The eternity of man depends on it.

Stories like this shouldn't scare us but compel us with great compassion towards a hurting humanity. Use this window called life to change the eternal course of the folks around you.

Father, I am honored that You would choose me to be a conduit of Your affection in this world. Today, empower me to go forth with divine urgency, seeing to it that the bride of Christ would be well prepared for the coming of the King. Jesus, You are returning for a spotless bride. Let me be a key player in removing every wrinkle and blemish from her. I pray these things in Jesus' name, amen.

You're Ready

> All Scripture is given by inspiration of God, and is profitable for doctrine, for reproof, for correction, for instruction in righteousness, that the man of God may be complete, thoroughly equipped for every good work. (2 Timothy 3:16–17 NKJV)

Masses of believers have great trepidation at the idea of sharing their faith. Concerns, worries, and what-if's dominate the mind producing paralyzing fear, keeping the believer out of action and ineffective.

When you maximize your worries, you undermine how big God is. What if I don't know what to say? If you're born again, you know something about this Jesus … so tell it! Don't allow what you don't know to hinder you from sharing what you do know. You don't measure maturity by your knowledge. You measure maturity by your fruit.

Instead of fearing the possibility of being rejected, rejoice in the possibility of being accepted. It's important that we don't love our own lives unto death. Remember, it's not about you anymore. Your job isn't promoting yourself, it's dying to yourself. "Then He said to them all, 'If anyone desires to come after Me, let him deny himself, and take up his cross daily, and follow Me. For whoever desires to save his life will lose it, but whoever loses his life for My sake will save it'" (Luke 9:23–24 NKJV).

I challenge you, lose your reputation as a casual church goer and pick up the reputation of a radical Jesus lover.

Father, I know that You have qualified me, sanctified me, and ordained me to complete every good work. I believe that I'm ready to say what You want me to say. I don't know everything but what I do know, I shall proclaim. I'm humbled and honored at the privilege of representing You. In Jesus' name, amen.

The Word of Knowledge

> Now concerning spiritual gifts, brethren, I do not want
> you to be ignorant ... (1 Corinthians 12:1 NKJV)

Why would Paul want us to avoid ignorance in the subject of spiritual gifts? Because if there is anything that would keep us from employing the gifts, it's ignorance. I encourage you, purpose in your heart to bring the gifts of the Holy Spirit into play while ministering.

I have a custom while praying for people. As I pray, I listen for the voice of God toward their life. As you do this, you'll find yourself praying things which you didn't think to pray. You may even transition over into a prophetic anointing and begin to speak the Word of the Lord over them.

Once while street witnessing, a man I was speaking to was stunned when the Lord told me that he had 2 daughters and one of his children had need of healing. He knew at that moment that our team was truly being used of the Lord, knowing things that only

God Himself could reveal. From there, I was able to minister with an open door.

You see, when the world sees that you know things that only God knows, you then have credibility in their sight. That positions them to receive the gospel that you're about to impart, because they know you to be a legitimate vessel.

Jesus utilized the word of knowledge at the well in John chapter 4, and the woman replied, "Sir, I perceive that You are a prophet." Her heart was then open to the salvation message that came next.

Today, be bold and step into the gifts of God. There is no need to force anything, for the gifts are "as the Spirit wills." Let the Lord share pieces of His omnipotence with you as you set out to change the world.

Father, just as Your Word instructs, I desire spiritual gifts. I long to be used mightily in such gifting. Bring forth opportunity to speak into lives with accuracy by Your Holy Spirit. May this beautiful ministry edify the body of Christ and position the lost to believe in our King Jesus. I pray these things in Jesus' name, amen.

Access

> I do not pray that You should take them out of the world, but that You should keep them from the evil one. (John 17:15 NKJV)

Why do you suppose Jesus prayed that you and I would stay in the world? It's simple: so that you and I could change the world. You can't change what you don't have access to. In fact, God can't even change what He doesn't have access to. God can't change your heart if you refuse to give Him access to it. Remaining in this world means we have access, and having access means we have influence.

Many are fighting to get by and crawling through life in survival mode. God hasn't called us to survive the world. He has called us to change the world. God wants to use His children to access every level and every platform of society such as business, entertainment, education, and government. Today, ask yourself, where is my pulpit? What is my platform? The Lord is not limited to influencing from the church house on Sunday morning. He wills to invade every last facet of culture.

You may have access to realms of influence that no one else has. Never allow the devil to isolate you and your voice. To be severed from the world is to be outside the will of God. If we are the salt, then expect God to sprinkle His flavor across a dead and bland earth—here, there, and everywhere.

Father, I thank You for giving me access to the world in which I live. David said, 'What good will it do if I am dead? Will the dust tell of Your faithfulness?' Lord, I am alive to make You known. Grant admission to every area of society to Your people, I pray. May You open doors of influence which cannot be shut. I pray this in Jesus' name, amen.

DAY 22

Our Influential Heritage

> Ask of Me, and I will give You the nations for Your inheritance, and the ends of the earth as Your possession. (Psalm 2:8 NKJV)

Servants make wages. Sons receive inheritance. The difference is that one is earned and the other is free. The free inheritance that we've stepped into as sons and daughters is gigantic. In fact, nations (plural) are our inheritance. In Christ, your birthright is to see the uttermost parts of the earth won for Christ. Don't think small—God doesn't. To be an imitator of God means your plans must become grandiose.

It's the will of God that nations would be vulnerable to the influence of the church. Jesus wants our families won for the glory of the Father. He desires our cities to be won and regions to be taken for His kingdom. But that's only the start. The Son of Man has been lifted up and He is drawing the globe unto Himself (see John 12:32). If God tells you to ask for something—ask.

I encourage you today, ask God for the nations. Many presidents, prime ministers, kings, and queens are scattered throughout the nations in positions of leadership. Pray that the Lordship of Jesus would be introduced to them all. May God Himself be seated on the throne of every nation and in the hearts of every leader. Always remember, intercession is influence.

Father, I place the leaders of the nations before Your throne. Draw them in by Your Spirit and cause wisdom to be displayed in each of their decisions. Destroy anything in their lives which may not be of You and encourage anything that is of You. Let them be refreshed and renewed in the love of Jesus daily. Lord, I am asking You this day for the nations, as Your Word instructs. Let us take back every single country for the glory of God in Christ Jesus. I pray these things in Jesus' name, amen.

The Throne of Influence

> But God, who is rich in mercy, because of His great love with which He loved us, even when we were dead in trespasses, made us alive together with Christ 8 (by grace you have been saved), and raised us up together, and made us sit together in the heavenly places in Christ Jesus. (Ephesians 2:4–6 NKJV)

Jesus is seated at the right hand of the Father and has saved a seat for you also. When God saved you, He didn't sit you down in a chair—He placed you on a throne. When an enthroned person speaks, others listen.

I was once preaching in a prison to several inmates about eliminating self-destructive thinking and talking. I referenced being seated with Christ on His throne. Then as I was preaching, I heard this exact phrase in my belly so clearly: "It's hard to talk down to someone who's sitting on a throne." I paused and then relayed the Word of the Lord to the men; they were greatly blessed by it—as was I.

The truth is, we ought not to belittle ourselves. Being seated on the throne means you're positioned for influence. It doesn't mean that you lord over the lost and domineer over your fellow man. It means that you invite them to sit with you.

You've been situated in excellence. As a result, you have something to give the world that no other group can give. Be sure to tell your peers of this total victory provided in Christ. Our Lord will never be dethroned. He always wins. Share this victory everywhere you walk, that others might take part in this victory also. There is plenty of room on the throne of Christ for others to come and be seated. Will you give the world an invitation?

Father, I am completely humbled and honored that You have made me to sit with You. Help me to reign in pure and loving influence toward this generation. I desire that all men be seated on this throne and I know that You do also, for Your desire is that all men be saved. This day, I yield to Your will and look forward to seeing continued divine operation in my day to day life. In Jesus' name, amen.

DAY 24

Administering a Covenant of Health

> And these signs will follow those who believe: In My name they will cast out demons; they will speak with new tongues; they will take up serpents; and if they drink anything deadly, it will by no means hurt them; they will lay hands on the sick, and they will recover. (Mark 16:17 NKJV)

This prophetic word Jesus gave concerning New Testament ministry was given no expiration date. Some would say that the reason Jesus healed the sick was to give evidence of His divine nature, thus validating His Word. There may be truth in such reasoning, but it makes the ministry of Jesus sound very mechanical.

The truth is simple: Jesus healed the sick because He was in love with people. His love hasn't wavered nor has His will to heal. A person with a cane, walker, or crutches on the street is a marvelous opportunity for God to show Himself strong. This doesn't mean that people are an experiment or a test subject. All people, sick or healthy, are targets for the love of God. Don't ever leave Jesus the

Healer out of your evangelistic exploits. Be quick to believe for miracle healings and God's best.

On the streets of Montego Bay, I met a man who walked with a stiff leg. He was unable to bend at the knee. I knelt down and prayed a brief, simple prayer of healing. I told him to check it out. With shock in his eyes, he flexed his knee completely. He repeatedly thanked us. We rejoiced in such an extravagant miracle.

I believe that it is the will of God that these sorts of miracles be distributed daily in the earth. Simply believe and be followed by supernatural power. Will you open yourself to being used by the Miracle Maker today?

Father, I am after Your power. I don't want to simply share a message; I want to demonstrate Your awesome power for the purpose of people being loved, touched, changed, and saved by the gospel. Allow those who are sick and hurting with all sorts of physical ailments to cross paths with Your people, that we might present to them a Jesus who heals. Jesus, I believe that through Your body, You are still going about doing good, healing those who are oppressed of the devil. Use me today. I pray in Jesus' name, amen.

Modern Levites

> At that time the Lord separated the tribe of Levi to bear the ark of the covenant of the Lord, to stand before the Lord to minister to Him and to bless in His name, to this day. (Deuteronomy 10:8 NKJV)

Out of every tribe in the nation of Israel, the Levites had a unique responsibility which separated them from the rest. As the nation would move from place to place, the tribe of Levi carried the ark of God's covenant—the place of His presence. This tribe with Presence was positioned right in the center of the nation in marching order.

I believe this is a type of the believer today. It's the will of God that we carry His glory in and upon us. We don't just carry a message, we carry a Presence. Furthermore, His presence is to be the centerpiece of our tribes and nations. In the Old Testament, the Ark of the Covenant was stolen from Israel by the Philistines, bringing devastation to the country. One man heard of the news and fell off of his seat, broke his neck and died. Another woman went into labor and named the child Ichabod—literally meaning "inglorious" (see 1 Samuel 4). The entire ordeal was a national disaster.

The sad thing is that some folks have gone so far astray that if God's glory were to lift off of their lives, they wouldn't even be aware of it. For example, Samson had been so blinded by relationships that were not God ordained that when the anointing of God lifted off of his life, he didn't even notice (see Judges 16:20).

The presence of the Lord is attractive. I was once leaving the church after a Wednesday night service. Most people had left already, but I noticed one young man sitting in the corner by himself. I approached and asked what was going on. He wasn't lost. He wasn't waiting for a ride. He wasn't hanging around to receive counsel from anyone. He was staying simply because he felt a presence in the house of God that he didn't feel anywhere else—and he didn't want to leave it. He described it as "indescribable." He felt happy. He felt joy. He felt peace. He felt God. I sat with him and there he received salvation and I taught him how to carry the presence with him "out there." This particular individual is still faithfully living for Jesus to this day and enjoying God's presence.

Learn to value God's presence. Determine in your heart that ministry apart from God's glory is a futile man-made effort. Take note that the Spirit of the Lord is upon you because you have been anointed to carry out the task of touching this planet with Jesus.

Father, just as a horn of oil was poured out upon David from head to toe, may Your anointing saturate my being wholly and completely.

I long for a greater measure of Your presence to be experienced in my day-to-day life. As I encounter the people of this world today, help me to transfer Your very presence to them—that they would shine in Your glory also. I pray this in Jesus' name, amen.

DAY 26

Your First Responder

> Preach the word! Be ready in season and out of season ...
> (2 Timothy 4:2 NKJV)

Evangelism is a proactive venture. You are often the one knocking on doors, seeking opportunity, and searching out the lost. Jesus said, "I came to seek and save that which is lost." He didn't come to wait for the lost to show up at His door. Sometimes, however, opportunity presents itself "out of season" without a warning or a heads up. If you're ready—you'll respond. If you're not—you'll run. If we live by faith when things are smooth, we will respond in faith when things get rocky.

At age 20, I was driving home on a late summer day. As I approached an intersection, a young lady pulled out in front of me. I had absolutely no chance to stop, so I swerved to miss her. I lost control of my vehicle, and as I went off of the road, my car was guided perfectly between 2 sizable posts buried in the ground and my car suffered no damage. I hopped out of my vehicle with a smile on my face. I approached the lady who caused the incident—she was quite nervous. I reassured her that I was okay and so was my vehicle. I told her how amazing Jesus is and that He loved her. I hugged her and we went on our way. She seemed shocked at the response.

When I thought of the incident later, I realized that she was probably expecting frustration from me. "Didn't you see me? You could have been killed! What's wrong with you?" The reality is, we have got to be able to give people Jesus and not our frustration. Don't be quick to judge and slow to show mercy. The Bible says that mercy triumphs over judgment (see James 2:13). Be careful that you don't respond in the flesh to inconvenient circumstances. You could foil a God opportunity if you do. Your born again spirit must be the first responder—not your flesh. If the mercy of the Lord endures forever, how long does ours endure?

Today, will you be merciful as He is merciful? Remember that in challenging circumstances, God is more than interested in showing Himself strong.

Father, I thank You for capitalizing on the circumstances that life might hand me. I'm only satisfied if I am responding like Jesus would respond—nothing more and nothing less. I pray that You would assist me in living from my spirit man and never from my flesh. I pray these things in the name of Jesus, amen.

Going to the Uttermost

> Therefore He is also able to save to the uttermost those who come to God through Him, since He always lives to make intercession for them. (Hebrews 7:25 NKJV)

Jesus is able to save to the uttermost. This means that the worst of the worst, the meanest of mean, and the top sinners in the world are all vulnerable to salvation. The furthest person from God on the planet is still susceptible to encountering the love of our Father. Don't rule out a single individual. God has a way of raising up those whom you never thought would be saved—all the while, the wise in this age stand confounded and scratching their head (see 1 Corinthians 1:27). Who do you know that is farther from God than anyone else? If you can't envision them being saved, change your vision.

The reason that Jesus is able to save to the uttermost is because people are willing to go to the uttermost. The reason that He can save folks who are in the farthest corners of the earth is because somebody has said, "Yes! I will go to the farthest corners of the earth." God does what He does on the earth because the church says yes.

Do you know anyone who is living in the "uttermost"? Would you go and herald the good news, making no apology? Sometimes the gospel means doing dirty work down in the trenches of society. The world won't always be begging to get into the church. We'll be the ones going out and getting them in.

Father, I am amazed at how far You reach. In the same way that You snatched me out of the fire, I pray that You would send me to snatch others out of that same fire. I'm willing to go where You send me. Whether it's to the streets of my city or on the other side of the world—You have a yes from me, God. In Jesus' name, amen.

The Saints' Work of Ministry

> And He Himself gave some to be apostles, some prophets, some evangelists, and some pastors and teachers, for the equipping of the saints for the work of ministry, for the edifying of the body of Christ … (Ephesians 4:11–12 NKJV)

The saints are not to leave ministry up to church leaders. In fact, you the saint are to be equipped and then act on what you've been equipped with. If you leave soul winning just to the evangelist and other fivefold ministers, heaven will be much less populated than it should be. I love seeing salvation at the altar in church. I love seeing salvation in the city outside of a formal gathering just as much.

As a believer, you do not carry an inferior anointing to full time ministers. Your ministry is not an "extra" or a side project. The influence of the everyday believer is lifeblood to the church. Working a full time secular job doesn't limit your ministry capacity. In fact, you have access to people and places that a full time minister would not.

When I entered full time ministry, it did not take me long to start missing the thrill of Christ's influence in my secular jobs. In the Bible, Daniel worked a secular job for a king who was a lost sinner, yet this didn't cap his influence or cause him to lose his voice. Instead, Daniel capitalized on the position he was in and glorified Almighty God in the middle of it all.

Be a Daniel. Be someone who chooses to flow in your calling no matter where you are or who you're around.

Father, I thank You for equipping me to carry out the work of Your ministry. I declare that I carry an anointing that breaks yokes in my workplace. In the middle of secular activity and everyday duties, I will glorify You and bring You honor. May this be seen by all who encounter me, for Your glory. I pray these things in Jesus' name, amen.

Breaking the Ice

> I tell you, love your enemies. Help and give without expecting a return. You'll never—I promise—regret it. Live out this God-created identity the way our Father lives toward us, generously and graciously, even when we're at our worst. Our Father is kind; you be kind. (Luke 6:35–36 MSG)

The practicality of the gospel is sometimes overlooked. Approaching someone in love doesn't mean you need to approach them with a spiritual conversation. Applaud your co-workers for good performance. Tell people that they inspire you when they do. Give compliments to others. If you have a spouse, start there and continue the kindness toward all you encounter. Learn to recognize gifting in others and work at cultivating it. Christianity is practical. It's so simple you may have to get out of the deep end to understand it.

In John chapter 4, Jesus ministered on the street by starting an ordinary conversation with a woman at the well. What was His ice breaker? "Would you give me a drink of water?" From there,

He was able to segue the conversation into talk of "living water," operate in word of knowledge, and minister life to the woman. It all started with a very natural and practical conversation.

Don't feel pressured to jump into the Bible a minute after you meet someone. The Lord is quite smooth in His dealings. A very practical and effective ice breaker that I have discovered is utilizing tattoos. So many in our culture display ink on their skin openly. Ask them, "What does that tattoo mean?"

Usually people get tattoos of things that are near and dear to their heart. This opens a door to you sharing the One who is near to your heart.

You don't have to shake hands with a person and immediately hand them a tract with a salvation message on it. Learn to flow in simple love towards others. God has a way of opening doors in conversation for the King to walk in and make Himself known.

Father, I pray that You would help me to be the most practical Christian I can be. I believe that I carry a useful, helpful gospel message. Help us as the body of Christ relate to the world—to weep with those who weep and rejoice with those who rejoice. I want to carry Your heart for the world around me. Give us wisdom in approaching others and refine our techniques. I thank You that everything is being done in nothing less than pure love. In Jesus' name, amen.

Preaching to Principalities

> To me, who am less than the least of all the saints, this grace was given, that I should preach among the Gentiles the unsearchable riches of Christ, and to make all see what is the fellowship of the mystery, which from the beginning of the ages has been hidden in God who created all things through Jesus Christ; to the intent that now the manifold wisdom of God might be made known by the church to the principalities and powers in the heavenly places, according to the eternal purpose which He accomplished in Christ Jesus our Lord ... (Ephesians 3:8–11 NKJV)

The apostle Paul had a way of packing tons of information into lengthy run-on sentences. It's important that we break down these passages and unpack them to gain understanding, for in all our getting—we are getting understanding. Essentially, Paul says: I have been graced and equipped to preach and reveal the mystery of God ... and here's why: so the great wisdom of God will be shown to the principalities, powers, and demons that are in the air. And guess who will be showing them—the church!

When you're preaching and sharing the gospel, you're not just preaching to the people in front of you ... you are preaching to the principalities, powers, and demonic forces of this age. Remember, Jesus didn't say go preach the gospel to just every person. He said preach the gospel to every "creature." It's true: heaven, hades, and the earth will all hear what the church has to say. The Lord God is using you to pour out judgment on the kingdom of darkness.

Today, be mindful of the power within the message that you bear. Open your mouth, because many are listening.

Father, thank You that Your foreknowledge and manifold wisdom is dropping the jaws of many. I am amazed that You would permit me to reveal such a marvelous mystery to this generation. May we carry out this task with the perfection of Christ in mind. Without fail, You are faithful, O Lord, and I give You thanks. In Jesus' name, amen.

Entrusted with Him

> He who is faithful in what is least is faithful also in much; and he who is unjust in what is least is unjust also in much. (Luke 16:10 NKJV)

The Lord has entrusted us with His best. We haven't been made ministers of a dry, mediocre covenant to mankind. We have been made ministers of the very person of Jesus Christ. God has such confidence in His sanctifying work in you, that He has delegated the most valuable riches that He has to you. The Father wants to position us so that we are able to be trusted with much.

Lives can be changed over a cup of coffee and Jesus. You don't always need a spiritual atmosphere; you need the One who abides in you. I once sat in a coffee shop with a young man who began to tell me that he was struggling with temptation to steal money from his father's business. In the past, he was the type of person who couldn't be trusted with money. You wouldn't want to leave your wallet around him —he'd be sure to search through it.

As I listened, the Holy Ghost told me just what to do. I said to him, "You're a different man now and this temptation is nothing. I can prove it to you." He looked interested. In my wallet, I had a significant amount of cash which I was taking on an international trip—it was important money. I handed it over to him and told him, "I am letting you watch this money for me. You're not going to spend it. You're not going to mess with it. You're just going to keep it for me." I told him the exact date that I wanted it back and in full. The date came and he handed me back exactly what I have given him—unaltered. I set out to prove to him that he was worthy to be trusted with finances. It may seem like an insignificant act, but being trusted with little qualifies you to be trusted with much.

What could God comfortably place in your hand? How much could He trust you with? I believe that the Lord is willing to give such vast resources to His church, but He sometimes withholds, knowing that those resources would become an idol to so many.

Don't pray for a million dollars if you know that a million dollar blessing would destroy you. Steward well the time, resources, finances, and influence that you currently have. If you want more lives to influence, do well with the smaller number that you have in front of you today. God will cause your voice to be heard by many in the future as you do well with the few in your present.

Father, I want to be able to be trusted with so much. Help me to be effective in properly stewarding the lives which I currently touch and speak into. As I do what You do and say what You say, increase my borders and expand my horizons. Holy Spirit, speak through me this day. I want the Word of God and not the will of man. I pray this in Jesus' name, amen.

Out of Control & Into Influence

> Let nothing be done through selfish ambition or conceit ...
> (Philippians 2:3 NKJV)

I once heard a preacher say, "You can't pray for God to change your spouse so that you have a better day. You pray for your spouse because you see the value of your spouse." If we just want folks around us saved so that we have less of a headache—that's a selfish prayer. Faith doesn't work through selfishness. Faith works through love (see Galatians 5:6).

God has taught me to pray for others for their sake, purifying myself of any selfish motive. If we attempt to change people apart from love, we are departing from godly influence and moving over into manipulation. Never slip into the idea that you can control people. God's authority to trample on serpents and scorpions has been given to you, but I want to remind you—your loved ones aren't serpents and scorpions. We aren't to walk on or manipulate others. People are beyond your control, but they are not beyond your influence. Set a visible example with your actions. The greatest testimony you can leave isn't always what you preach but what you flesh out.

Forcing folks into the kingdom is never a biblical concept—it can't be done. Bribery isn't a method by which folks obtain salvation. Our position is to step out of control and into influence. Being willing to present truth, sway hearts, and watch as God seals the deal.

Father, I want to offer prayer to You that is completely fueled by a heart of love. I want all that I do to be done in Your very love. Help me to be an ideal example of what a Jesus follower looks like. My job isn't to bend the arm of another so that they receive Jesus. My job is to influence with a loving heart. My desire is to please You, Lord. Thank You for who You are. In Jesus' name, amen.

DAY 33

Sticking with the Superior

> Therefore when Jesus perceived that they were about to come and take Him by force to make Him king, He departed again to the mountain by Himself alone. (John 6:15 NKJV)

The nation of Israel wanted to make Jesus their King. In the natural, being the highest political figure in the land would seem to be the place of maximum influence. However, the route to maximum influence was the blood trickled trail called Via Dolorosa—the Way of Sorrows. In John 6, Jesus rejected earthly promotion in order to stay in the place of the Father's perfect will. The nation wanted to place Him on the throne right then and there, but He knew that He had a much better heavenly throne waiting on Him. Don't settle for an inferior promise because you lack the patience to wait for the superior one.

Often times, our idea of influence means having a million followers and the power to hire and fire. God's idea of influence is the less traveled path of humility and lowliness of mind. Great men and women of God have turned down remarkable earthly promotion and opportunity in order to fulfill a divine mandate. Sometimes we must sacrifice job security and comfort on the altar of absolute obedience.

If you believe God has called you to a certain task, don't quit unless He gives new orders. If you believe the Lord has positioned you in a specific region, don't leave until you hear Him relocate you. Are there any earthly promotions or opportunities that you need to decline in order to remain in God's will? I want to encourage you, the cost of being in the perfect plan of God is never too much, no matter the size of the sacrifice.

Father, I thank You for the power to travel the lowly path of humility. I know by Your Word that humility is the place of influence. I believe that promotion comes from You, and I thank You that when I turn down certain opportunities for the Kingdom's sake, You will meet me with an even better and fresher opportunity shortly. I love You and trust You, my King. I pray this in Jesus' name, amen.

DAY 34

Agreeability

> Agree with your adversary quickly, while you are on the way with him, lest your adversary deliver you to the judge, the judge hand you over to the officer, and you be thrown into prison. (Matthew 5:25 NKJV)

In conversation with another, don't intentionally search for phrases and statements that you disagree with or wish to refute. Love searches for common ground. Love believes all things and hopes all things. People don't get saved because you make a sharp point or put up a good argument. People get saved because the Father draws them into His Son (see John 6:44).

Sadly, many are bent on seeking a debate rather than unity. Jesus was approached with questions which were geared at tripping Him up. That same spirit is in operation today. Immaturity focuses on differences where as love unifies.

The greatest case that you can make for your faith is a life lived by faith. Your life should be an altar call to the world around you. Is your lifestyle inviting the lost into the knowledge of a loving Savior or is it repelling the lost away from God and His church?

Father, I honor You and Your reign over me. I want to live as someone who is a stranger to quarrelling. I have no reason to include myself in a mean spirited debate. I am asking that You would aid me in living a life by faith which invites my contemporaries into Your truth. We know that You are interested in winning souls, not arguments. Let us live from that place of love, O Lord. I pray this in Jesus' mighty name, amen.

Riding at Night

> Then I arose in the night, I and a few men with me; I told no one what my God had put in my heart to do at Jerusalem; nor was there any animal with me, except the one on which I rode. And I went out by night through the Valley Gate to the Serpent Well and the Refuse Gate, and viewed the walls of Jerusalem which were broken down and its gates which were burned with fire. (Nehemiah 2:12–13 NKJV)

Growing up, my dad would continually tell me that leadership is a lonely place. Leaders do what followers won't—that's why they are leaders. In this beautiful story, Nehemiah was leading a project to rebuild the walls of his beloved city Jerusalem.

As he set out to assess the damage in chapter 2, it was a lonely ride but a necessary ride. Influencers are willing to work when others sleep. Influencers are willing to confront the damage that others may avoid. We often times pray and believe God that we will see heaven on earth. It's a great prayer, but in reality, if we want to see heaven on earth, we must make room for heaven on earth.

Like Nehemiah, you will be given opportunity to assess the damage of various situations. Never just assess the damage, but prophecy the restoration. Business schools teach a sound principle: in a meeting, don't bring a problem to the table without bringing a solution. What sort of chaos might God place you in the middle of to bring about a turnaround? Are there broken and destroyed walls in your life or the life of another for you to rebuild?

Today, lead the influence to see health and restoration manifested.

Father, I am willing to evaluate the issues which need to be addressed in my life, in my family, and in my city. As I set out to behold these matters, help me to behold the solutions as well. Send me out. Even if no one else will go, I will go. Thank You, Lord, for gracing me with every good thing I need to perform and carry out every good work for Your name's sake. I pray this in the wonderful name of Jesus Christ, amen.

Gaining Entrance

> ...These things says He who is holy, He who is true, 'He who has the key of David, He who opens and no one shuts, and shuts and no one opens.' (Revelation 3:7 NKJV)

No single sector of society is unreachable. If you have Jesus, you always have an "in." Our job is not to just see mankind touched inside the doors of the church. We also have a mandate to penetrate kingdoms, cultures, and every single people group with the influence of Almighty God. There are people who will simply never come to church. This doesn't thwart our purpose or plan. It's simple: the church must go to them.

Many have God-given dreams and aspirations to advance in areas like international business, graphic design, sports, financial advising, mechanics, music, and so forth. God wants to propel the church in all of these realms, that the unreached, unchurched, and ungodly would experience an excellent church representing a perfect Jesus.

The Lord isn't so limited that He only anoints preachers. No, if you're a believer, you have an anointing—period (see 1 John 2:20). What unique anointing is upon your life? Are there unusual avenues of influence that the Lord could use you in that you haven't considered?

Be encouraged. Dream again! See to it that you infect your generation with the gospel on every level.

Father, I thank You for continually filling me with the Holy Spirit. I need more and more of You. Use me in distinctive ways within the family, business, and cultures You've placed me in. I want an increased anointing upon my life, that an increased influence would be evident. Send me to the unreached, for it's Your desire that all be saved. I pray these things in the name of Your Son Jesus, amen.

Undeniable and Incomprehensible

Look among the nations and watch—Be utterly astounded!
For I will work a work in your days which you would not
believe, though it were told you. (Habakkuk 1:5 NKJV)

The Bible starts with a powerful display of the Lord's awesome creativity. Lights, waters, sky, herbs, animals—all called into being by the Word of God. From there, God continues to show off His powerful nature with the salvation of Noah, Abraham's exploits, Joseph's rise to authority, the Red Sea's split with Moses, Joshua's relentless military campaign, Gideon doing the impossible, David obtaining kingship and beheading the enemy, Solomon's wisdom and riches, Elijah's adventurous power-packed ministry, the prophets' fiery messages to the nation, the entrance of King Jesus, the great altar called Calvary, the glorious resurrection, the fire-filled upper room, and the miracle-littered ministry of the early church.

God is still dropping jaws today. We have a God who is ever active in doing the impossible and granting miracles according to our faith. I don't have the ability to perform a miracle. It's never according to my power. However, it is according to my faith (see Matthew 9:29).

Your faith has the ability to access the power of our Miracle Maker. Don't think that the grandiose acts of God have expired. His acts aren't gone. They're available. Reflect on the size of God and laugh at the opposition. Jesus wants to display Himself in ways that people won't be able to deny. They may be able to resent it—but they can't deny it.

People in your very community are stuck between Egyptians and the Red Sea. Will you believe God for the miraculous? Will you refuse to relent until you see your community pass through the sea on dry land? God's big enough. Is your willingness to believe Him big enough?

Father God, I am believing You for the impossible. I want to see the outrageous and awesome acts of God displayed in my community. Come and make Yourself known. Show off Your powerful deeds of love and mercy. Through Your miraculous nature, let Jesus be lifted up—drawing all men unto Himself. I pray these things in Jesus' name, amen.

Your Ministry of Connections

> Now all things are of God, who has reconciled us to Himself through Jesus Christ, and has given us the ministry of reconciliation ... (2 Corinthians 5:18 NKJV)

According to 2 Corinthians, you and I have a ministry—a ministry to connect man with God. Does that mean that God is about to give you a pulpit, a building, a website, and a worldwide itinerate ministry? Probably not. For some He may give that calling, but typically, your career is your ministry. Your 9 to 5 is your platform. Never detest secular work; instead, embrace it! God has not only given you a ministry but He has given you a very specific place to carry out that ministry. The Lord is very intentional in His placement of people—never discount that.

I was once riding in the back of an ambulance after a bad car accident making conversation with the pleasant first responder who was caring for me. She was a Christian who was new to working in this particular area. As I lay on the stretcher I said to her, "I can see that this isn't just a job for you—it's a ministry."

The world needs many things, and reconciliation to a loving Father is at the very top of the list. You are the one walking in such ministry. Develop it, grow in it, and explore God's love and might in your very ministry.

Father, I give You thanks for the ministry that You have bestowed upon me. My dream is to see the world reconciled and permanently connected to You, our dear Father—through Jesus Christ. Flow, flow, and flow some more through this vessel, I pray. I long to witness mass reconciliation in the world around me. I pray these things in faith. In Jesus' name, amen.

Living the Dream

Then he dreamed still another dream … (Genesis 37:9 NKJV)

Joseph was a man who dreamed. Because he was a man who dreamed, he became a man who achieved. Without dreams, visions, and goals, you don't live to fulfill a thing. When your purpose is unfulfilled, you yourself are unfulfilled. This is truly tragic. A dormant dream is not a dream, it's a nightmare. We long to be a people who dream big, knowing that God is able to finish what He has started in us (see Philippians 1:6). Let's transition from dreaming the dream to living the dream.

In the Kingdom of God, a dream is always about more folks than just you. Often times, we talk about our "vision," but our vision must not be a man-made plan to fulfill a self-centered ambition. Your goals must be centered on the influence of somebody else. Is it wrong to have dreams and plans for yourself? Of course not! However, if your dream is reduced to you only, you're looking through a self-centered lens of the future which lacks fulfillment and selfless luster. Write or type your vision out plain as Habakkuk

2:2 instructs, and when you do, be sure to include many others apart from yourself. You are destined for influence.

The Lord loves to schedule appointments for us. Your future has meetings set up between you and others who need to hear your heart. Let your personal vision be one that houses eternal impact. Develop strategies that don't just meet your need of personal provision but meet the need of a hurting humanity.

Father, I thank You that in the last days we shall dream dreams. May my dreams be full of godly influence. My priority isn't self fulfillment or making sure that I have all of my ducks in a row. My focus is fulfilling a selfless vision of love according to Your perfect will. May You make the proper connections and alignments, that I would live the dream that You are birthing in my heart. In Jesus' precious name, amen.

The Cross: A Practical Approach

> And I, brethren, if I still preach circumcision, why do I still suffer persecution? Then the offense of the cross has ceased. (Galatians 5:11 NKJV)

The cross is offensive. How do you comfortably dive into an offensive subject with strangers while witnessing? In our culture, the cross is worn around the necks of people who don't know what it means. Sinners wear crosses. This makes for a practical approach. Upon seeing someone with a crucifix on their neck, ask them, "Why do you wear that?" or "What does the cross mean to you?"

People are willing to publically display the cross; why not publically confess what it means? Jesus disarmed principalities and powers, and made a public spectacle of them (see Colossians 2:15). The cross is world famous and known globally. It's the pinnacle of the human experience. It's the centerpiece of our message. This beautiful cross around necks and tattooed on the skin of many—be quick to reference it. "Breaking the ice" is one of the great challenges of ministering in the streets. The cross might just be your way in.

Father, I honor You and thank You for the cross. I understand that upon this great altar, You were laid, Jesus—willingly laying down Your life that I would be saved. Following this cross, You were raised for my justification. You were seated on the throne so I could sit with You. I pray that You would use me to impart this understanding of the cross to those who don't have it. I don't want to see the world displaying a cross that they don't understand. I want to see the world displaying a cross which they have come to, in repentance, to receive Your great salvation, O God. I pray these things in the name of the Lord Jesus Christ of Nazareth, amen.

To Please or to Love

> For do I now persuade men, or God? Or do I seek to please men? For if I still pleased men, I would not be a bondservant of Christ. (Galatians 1:10 NKJV)

The Message Bible renders this passage, "If my goal was popularity, I wouldn't bother being Christ's slave." Do we want to be popular or do we want to be effective?

Your job as a Christian isn't to please the world. Your job is to love the world. There is a stark difference between the two. You could probably find a self-centered, demon possessed drug dealer who pleases people without ever loving people. Your fixation isn't pleasing people.

Does this mean that your goal is to offend or make people angry? Of course not! Never allow a spirit of pride to attach itself to your theology. We aren't trying to offend people and make them angry, but at the same time, we aren't desperate for their approval—we are desperate for His. This mentality will take your far. Religious pride with strip you of your influence and rob you of your effectiveness in ministry.

We are calling the wrong thing "Lord" if we allow the compromise that's in this world to compromise the gospel that we preach. Always bow your knee to the Lamb who is on the throne forever, not an impulse to please the crowd with political correctness. On that same note, this gospel must be shared in a spirit of love— otherwise, it's nothing but a pushy sales pitch.

Remember today that you won't please everyone. If you do, you probably aren't being Christ-like. Aim for love in all things and the Lord will abound through you to maximize your impact in the earth.

Father, I thank You that my purpose is love. It's the reason that I have breath in my lungs. You aren't obsessed with pleasing people—and I won't be either. I seek to do Your will by manifesting Your truth in love. Right now, I lay down my life, take up my cross, and Jesus—I'm coming after You. I've got the Holy Ghost in and on me, I've got fire in my heart, I've got God on my mind—Lord, use me! I pray these things in the awesome name of Jesus, amen.

A Holy Burden

> Carry each other's burdens, and in this way you will fulfill the law of Christ. (Galatians 6:2 NIV)

In the Old Testament, when a message from the Lord was received by a prophet, it was often described as a "burden" (see Nahum 1:1 and Isaiah 13:1). The Word of the Lord deposited into you bears a certain weight. The only way of releasing that weight is by speaking it out. This is why Jeremiah so famously uttered, "his word is in my heart like a fire, a fire shut up in my bones. I am weary of holding it in; indeed, I cannot.." (Jeremiah 20:9 NIV)

The church must carry heaven's holy burden for the lost. I want to carry a godly heaviness for the world around me. Not a heaviness that drags me down, but one that compels me to action, intercession, and influence.

Allow yourself to be touched by the pain of someone else. Cry with those who cry and laugh with those who laugh. Many in the church have grown cold to the infirmities running rampant in their sphere of influence. Be sensitive to the depravities and needs of humanity. Carry a belly aching intercession for the lost.

In your Bible, the word "compassion" means "to suffer with." Millions are carrying a weight which they cannot manage on their own. Will you be someone to alleviate their burden or someone who adds to their burden?

Father, I want to feel Your heart on every level. I want to sympathize with Your people and help bear their weight in order to see that weight lifted. I'm ready to intercede for and touch the downtrodden. Release to me the righteous burden of Your Word, O Lord. I pray these things in Jesus' name, amen.

The Lost are Lost

…whose minds the god of this age has blinded, who do not believe, lest the light of the gospel of the glory of Christ, who is the image of God, should shine on them. (2 Corinthians 4:4 NKJV)

Be careful that you don't heed the lie that a sin- filled life is something to be desired. Refuse to walk with a sense that you're somehow "missing out" by living in the straight line called righteousness.

Shortly after getting saved, I was working at a plaza in my hometown. During my work shift, I saw a man who was staying with a woman he wasn't married to. They were on the drunken side of things and seemed to be having an awesome time. I remember I had this thought, "See, they're living in sin … and they are doing just fine and having a great time." This guy seemed to have it all together, but remember, the lost are just that—lost. The devil wants you to take note of the bait without ever noticing the hook.

At the end of that work shift, I clocked out and began driving home. As I drove home, the Lord told me to go back and minister to that man. It was such a strong and urgent conviction that I turned the car around immediately. I went back to the place I last saw him and sure enough, he was there. I don't even remember what I said as I approached him, but within seconds he was crying. I wasn't staring at a sinner who was having the time of his life and loving it. I was looking at a broken man who was crying out for help. His marriage was destroyed, alcoholism was gripping his life, he was going from woman to woman to fill a void, and so forth. I was able to minister life to him for almost an hour, when he confessed that Jesus was the only way and was absolutely floored by the divine appointment.

I learned that the lost may wear a smile on the outside while crying out for help on the inside. So many who live in sin don't want to stay in sin but yearn to get out. You're the messenger whom God is sending. I encourage you, answer the call.

Father, I glorify You and honor Your name. I see that the pleasure of sin is temporary and fading. Your peace and joy endure for always. Help me to reach into the fire and snatch Your people out. Many are crying out for an answer and I believe that the Answer lives within my spirit. I'm willing to go where You send me, Father. I'm excited for the exploits that You're sending me on in this season! I pray this in the great name of Jesus Christ of Nazareth, amen.

Lost Sons and Daughters

And he arose and came to his father. But when he was still a great way off, his father saw him and had compassion, and ran and fell on his neck and kissed him. (Luke 15:20 NKJV)

We all know folks who are a great way off. Are we running to them or neglecting them? The father in Luke 15 didn't wait at the door with an "I told you so" attitude. He embraced the son with love unconditional. We are witnessing days now where masses of lost sons and daughters are making their way home. Be a home that lost children can return to. The world should know that the church will embrace, not condemn.

Live with a hopeful expectation that the lost are coming back. Many fret, fear, and worry over the backslidden. You can't allow someone's damnation to steal from your salvation. That isn't a lack of compassion. It's refusing to allow the devil to capitalize on a situation that's already rough. There is a time to carry a burden and hurt for people—but another person's wickedness doesn't give you permission to drag your way through life week after week, month after month, or even year after year. Nothing in this world has the right or the authority to put a cap on your influence.

Prophesy over your future that the days are near where you will fall on the neck of many lost children with the very embrace of Jesus.

Father God, I am pursuing the lost and backslidden through my intercession, my witness, and my example. Enable me to notice those who are far off and quicken me to run after them with a loving welcome into Your Kingdom. I prophesy according to Your Word that I shall embrace many and welcome them into the lifestyle that You have ordained for them, Lord God. I thank You for letting these things come to pass. In the righteous name of the Lord Jesus, amen.

DAY 45

Ministering Out of Him

> "...The words that I speak to you I do not speak on My own authority; but the Father who dwells in Me does the works. (John 14:10 NKJV)

Live desperate for the anointing of God. The Lord once spoke to me, "The only way that you would feel under pressure is if you are still running the show." When we lean not on ourselves but on the anointing of the Spirit of God, the pressure is alleviated because God Himself takes the responsibility. It's a simple trust transfer that must take place in the minds and hearts of Christians. If I start to feel antsy or nervous before preaching, I will remind myself, "I'm not under pressure. It's not my performance. It's Christ in me who is doing the thing."

As a vessel, you don't have anything to offer. The only thing you have to offer is whatever you're being filled with. Thank God that we are filled beyond the brim with the precious Holy Ghost. As you set out to love people, you aren't ministering out of your own resources. You are leaning on an anointing that's bigger than you. It's not about your ability to put together a perfect presentation of truth or pin down every step for ideal influence. It's all about your ability to yield to the Greater One within you who is more than able to perform. God has everything to do with it.

Ministry without dependency upon Holy Spirit is a man-made religious production at best. Be somebody who draws from the unlimited well of living water which was promised to you by Christ.

Father, You are my Father. I'm in love with You. If I minister out of my own strength and creativity, I will fall on my face in a hurry. I need Your wonderful anointing to empower me to do what I cannot do alone. Let me minister out of You always, Lord. I'm not interested in self-help. I'm interested in God-help. Continue to show Yourself strong in my life as I yield to You, O God. I pray this prayer in the holy name of Jesus Christ, amen.

Generosity's Impact

> Give freely and become more wealthy; be stingy and lose everything. (Proverbs 11:24 NLT)

I know a woman who was a waitress in college. She was waiting on a table of people who were Christians, apparently. The problem is that they were a headache to deal with. The table had several people, they were very demanding, not pleasant to work with, and their bill at the end of the meal was for over $100. It was the sort of situation where their tip should be quite generous. When it came time to leave a tip, they didn't leave a tip. Instead, they left a little New Testament Bible—and that's it.

Perhaps the table would have benefited from opening that Bible and reading Scriptures on generosity. If they were trying to slap the waitress in the face, they did an excellent job of it. I'm not against giving people the Word of God, but I am against stinginess. Stinginess is a horrible representation of a giving God. Love isn't tightfisted. Love freely gives. These folks could have paired the Bible with a $20 or $50 and left that on the table. Then suddenly generosity becomes the strength behind the witness. Then the waitress sees that God so loved the world that He gave His Son, and she can believe that because the church so loves the world that they give a decent tip.

Your generosity speaks in a volume that might be louder than you even realize. The world has seen enough of a hypocritical and judgmental church. Will you rise up by the power of God and clean up the image of this imperfect yet beautiful bride called the church?

Learn to operate in generosity as a lifestyle. As you do, the gospel you preach and the Word you share will have credibility in the sight of those who listen.

Father, this day I make generosity a core value in my life. I am blessed coming in and going out, beyond measure and comprehension. I have something to give those in need. I have enough to share. Give forth opportunity to bless the world with abundance. Lord God, You have never been tightfisted with me, therefore I refuse to be tightfisted toward the world. I thank You and look forward to awesome influence in the vein of generosity—all for Your glory. In Jesus' name, amen.

Maximum Impact

> Then Jesus returned in the power of the Spirit to Galilee,
> and news of Him went out through all the surrounding
> region. (Luke 4:14 NKJV)

Christ didn't have a 50 year ministry spanning for decades and
decades. He had a 3 year window of opportunity. With a short
ministry duration, God was sure to make the most of the time
and provide maximum impact to the world.

You and I don't have forever here. The earth isn't our home; it's a
visitation place. The Bible says that people of faith confessed that
they were "strangers and pilgrims on the earth" (Hebrews 11:13
NKJV). Our time is limited, but our impact doesn't have to be.

"And do this, knowing the time, that now it is high time to awake
out of sleep; for now our salvation is nearer than when we first
believed. The night is far spent, the day is at hand. Therefore let
us cast off the works of darkness, and let us put on the armor of
light" (Romans 13:11–12 NKJV).

With the Day of the Lord approaching, our influence must be intentional. Our display of Christ isn't to be sporadic, inconsistent, or sloppy. With effectiveness in mind, we ought to move into the society around us with a deliberate goal of manifesting the Kingdom of God day after day. Godly influence should never take a hiatus from your lifestyle.

Pray and prepare for the work that God would cause you to set your hand to. Cling to zeal and reject apathy, for our time is temporary, but our impact is eternal.

Father, I bless You. Enable us to make the most of this small window of opportunity that we have on the earth. I don't want to depart from the earth with a halfway completed assignment. I yearn to experience the fullness of the mission and mandate which You've placed within my heart and soul. Like Jesus, may I do more in my ministering than what can even be contained in the pages of a book. I call these things completed, in Jesus' name, amen.

Insufficient, Inferior, and Inadequate

> So he said to Him, 'O my Lord, how can I save Israel? Indeed my clan is the weakest in Manasseh, and I am the least in my father's house.' (Judges 6:15 NKJV)

Insufficient means "not enough," inferior means "lower in rank or status," and inadequate means "lacking in quality or quantity." When we compare ourselves to the size of our God-given assignment, we may feel that these 3 words describe us quite well.

The good news is that these 3 words don't describe our God. He is an all-sufficient Savior who gives us more than enough. He is a superior God who has seated us with Jesus at His right hand with no sense of inferiority to people or the things of this world. He is a perfectly adequate God, and as we seek Him, we are promised to lack no good thing (see Psalm 34:10).

In Judges 5, Gideon was living in an all time low. He was the least of the least, yet God ordained him to save the nation. Not just a family, a people group, or a region—but a nation. Biblically, the Lord shows interest in those who don't have what it takes. God shows off best when He is using folks who don't have anything to offer on their own. With the help and favor of the Lord God, Gideon obeyed, acted, and succeeded. A national salvation took place not because Gideon had credentials and qualifications, but because Gideon had Jehovah God.

If you're going to take a look at your own insufficiency, be sure to take a longer look at His complete sufficiency. If you're going to speak of your own inferiority, speak louder about the superiority of the one true living God. If you're going to mention your own inadequacies, be sure to major on the brilliantly adequate God who saved you.

Father, I honor Your name. I've come to believe with my whole heart that You're more than enough. Completely sufficient for me. As I expose my weakness to You, reveal Your strength to me. Like Gideon, send me out today to do the impossible. I won't reach satisfaction until I am operating in the fullness of the influence You've set in front of me. I pray this in Jesus' mighty name, amen.

Refusing the Great Debate

> And a servant of the Lord must not quarrel but be gentle
> to all, able to teach, patient … (2 Timothy 2:24 NKJV)

The Holy Ghost doesn't cooperate with an argumentative spirit.
Love believes all things and hopes all things. Many walk with
stones in their hands ready to throw them at anyone who violates
their doctrine. May that never be our position.

Too often, Christians are known for their ability to debate instead
of their ability to love. Prove the superiority of faith in Christ by
being quick to display it while refusing to argue it. There is a time
to reason and persuade, but never a time to be quarrelsome. A
"critic" is not a new testament ministry.

The religious crowd in the days of Jesus were bent on making
points and asking questions to get Him backpedaling. We don't
have record that Jesus ever locked into any verbal boxing matches.
Rather, He would give simple, God-inspired answers or even
answer questions with a question.

Nonbelievers are notorious for targeting Christians with an argumentative, Pharisee-mindset in the workplace. Responding in the flesh won't change the other person. Giving heavens response will do that.

Father, I thank You that I am slow to speak but quick to listen. I refuse to be ensnared and caught up in long, drawn out arguments. Those things are unprofitable to me and the other person involved. It's not about me winning a debate. It's about You winning their hearts. Today, I believe that I have sufficient patience from You to do Your will with precision and accuracy. In Jesus' holy name, amen.

Endless Oil

> So she went from him and shut the door behind her and her sons, who brought the vessels to her; and she poured it out. Now it came to pass, when the vessels were full, that she said to her son, "Bring me another vessel ..." (2 Kings 4:5–6 NKJV)

God will honor any seed that you sow by increasing it and handing it back to you. Good works are not forgotten by God. They're rewarded by God.

In 2 Kings, the oil wasn't multiplied until the oil was poured out. Many are crying out, "Lord increase the anointing upon my life!" Yet, increased anointing doesn't come through increased begging. More oil comes by pouring out what you have.

The anointing doesn't increase *so that* you can do ministry. The anointing increases *as* you do ministry. This is the order of the Lord.

God counts every dollar that you sow. He keeps track of every second of time that you give. He measures every ounce of influence that you pour out and is sure to reward it. Jesus adds interest to the things we dish out. Our purpose isn't to do good solely to receive a reward. "Giving to get" is a selfish concept. I believe that it often is a "spiritual" mask for covetousness. Many have embraced doctrinal ideas that promote selfishness and reinforce narcissism. At the same time, to neglect reward is to neglect God's will. Rejecting a harvest is undermining the purpose of the seed.

Today, freely scatter the seed of influence in the field of the world around you, not forgetting that a rewarding harvest is on its way the second that seed hits the soil.

Father, this day I will to do good to all—whether it's leaving a generous tip or mowing my neighbors lawn. You are in the business of acts of kindness; therefore, I am also. Enable me and empower me this day to recognize opportune times to sow seed and plant loving kindness into the lives around me. I trust You and honor You, O Lord. I pray these things in the magnificent name of Jesus, amen.

DAY 51

Stagnant Authority is No Authority

> Behold, I give you the authority to trample on serpents and scorpions, and over all the power of the enemy, and nothing shall by any means hurt you. (Luke 10:19 NKJV)

As the body of Jesus, we have a spiritual authority that I'm convinced we don't use enough. In the Garden of Eden, we see the first spiritual battle launched against mankind. Do you realize that when the serpent showed up in Genesis 3, Eve could have said, "I command that you flee from me" —and the serpent would have no choice but to flee? Why? Because of Genesis 1— the Lord God gave Adam and Eve dominion over every creeping thing that creeps on the earth. You had better believe that the serpent was included in that category.

Eve went wrong when she failed to operate in her God-given authority. Dominion does you nothing until you use it. Don't allow a serpent in your garden that doesn't belong there. You may be tempted with the forbidden fruit of keeping quiet. You may be tempted with the forbidden fruit of the fear of man. You may be tempted with the forbidden fruit of political correctness. Shake off the snake and stand on the Word of God to go and preach this gospel to every creature (see Mark 16:15).

Father, I thank You for Your very dominion resting upon me on this earth. I refuse to allow any unwanted serpent to disrupt the divine flow of influence through my life. Do what You want, Lord—I'm standing steadfast on Your eternal Word. I pray this in Jesus' name, amen.

Rejoicing in Rejection

> Blessed are you when they revile and persecute you, and say all kinds of evil against you falsely for My sake. Rejoice and be exceedingly glad, for great is your reward in heaven, for so they persecuted the prophets who were before you. (Matthew 5:11–12 NKJV)

I wish that everyone who heard the gospel would say yes to the gospel, but it's not so. We either let the filth and rejection cling to us or shake the dust off of our feet and move on with joy (see Matthew 10:14 and Acts 13:51–52). Learning to navigate rejection is a must in the world of witnessing.

I once approached a man in a park to share Christ. I struck up a very casual conversation—nothing spiritual whatsoever. With a completely angry countenance, he said to me, "Do I know you?" I told him that we didn't know one another and so he responded, "Then why are you talking to me?" I began to tell him that we were out encouraging folks and so forth. He shut me down completely and didn't want anything to do with it. He was so angry I thought he could have hit me. I walked away from the conversation with nothing to show for it. It's in these moments of rejection that we shouldn't be overcome with discouragement but fueled with compassion.

Many don't witness because they fear the possibility of being rejected. With this mindset, we are making it loud and clear that we are still in it for ourselves. Whether we are rejected or accepted, our message and mission stays the same.

Pray today that ears would be opened and hearts would be receptive. Pray that God would deal with the hearts of the cold and bitter. Set out to preach the Word and believe that the acceptance of the gospel would become more widespread than ever. Rejection isn't a setback for you. Rejection is fuel to reach further and pursue with greater fervency.

Lord, I trust that Your Word will not return void. Every time I declare it, I believe that it is seed into the lives of people—whether they heed it right away or not. I won't fear rejection. I will trust You, O God. Thank You for placing heaven's mandate within my spirit. May we have compassion on the world that's walking away from the cross. May Your love and Holy Spirit chase them down more and more, for the time is short. I pray such things in the precious name of the Son of God—Christ Jesus my Lord, amen.

A Magnetic Gospel

> ...He had no beauty or majesty to attract us to Him, nothing in His appearance that we should desire Him. (Isaiah 53:2 NIV)

Jesus had no outward beauty that we should behold Him. Yet everyone wanted to behold Him. There was nothing about His appearance that would draw a crowd. Yet the masses and multitudes flocked to Him.

From the fall of man to the cross, mankind had a dam in their relationship with God. From Jesus on, God has been reconciling the world back to Himself. " ...That is, that God was in Christ reconciling the world to Himself, not imputing their trespasses to them, and has committed to us the word of reconciliation" (2 Corinthians 5:19 NKJV). Through this new covenant, lost sons and daughters are being reconciled back to their Father. If Jesus be lifted up, He will draw all men unto Himself (see John 12:32). It's very simple: God currently has a magnet on the people of the earth, and He is pulling them in daily.

The Lord is touching people in an irresistible way. In Luke 21:15 NIV, Christ said to His disciples, "For I will give you words and wisdom that none of your adversaries will be able to resist or contradict." I have found that many people end up in churches and they don't know why, they were simply drawn in by the Spirit of God.

I remember once praying in the Spirit, and hearing God speak to me so clearly. I saw a picture of a big horseshoe shaped magnet. The Lord spoke to me that He has His magnet on people. Folks are being drawn in and they might not even know why. Many talk about the how relentlessly the devil pursues Christians to bait them into backsliding. I just believe in giving the relentlessness of God more credit than Satan.

Like Jesus, you and I may have nothing special to offer outwardly, yet people will come. The broken are attracted to people who can mend. The sick are attracted to those who heal. The hopeless are engrossed with a confident message of hope. Know today that many want what you have. It's your responsibility to tell them how to get it.

Father, this generation is longing to have what I have as a Christian. There is a void in the hearts of men and only You can fill it. I thank You that this message we have on our lips is attractive. It's something that will bring the masses close to You. Keep Your holy magnet on the hearts and minds of the people. Never let Your conviction relent or lift. As You have been relentless in Your pursuit of me, may I be relentless in my pursuit of the world. I pray this in the great name of Jesus Christ of Nazareth, amen.

Greater Works

> Most assuredly, I say to you, he who believes in Me, the works that I do he will do also; and greater works than these he will do, because I go to My Father. (John 14:12 NKJV)

Being Christ-like is the goal of our conversion. Being Christ-like isn't just living in the character of Jesus. It isn't just holding your tongue when you want to get angry or abstaining from immorality when temptation is on. Being Christ-like also means doing what Jesus did. It means laying hands on the sick, casting out demons, and declaring the Word of the Lord. By the grace of God, we must duplicate the character of Jesus, as well as duplicate the powerful works of Jesus.

It is the will of God that you and I do greater works than Jesus Himself. It's not impossible. It's remarkably plausible. Our heart cry should be to witness for ourselves the "greater works" which Jesus spoke of.

In the name of ministry, we sometimes go about works and outreach that have nothing to do with greater works. The model of our ministry isn't something we have to fabricate. Our ministry blueprint is presented in our Bible. Refuse to be satisfied with a powerless gospel. The life of Jesus had no shortage of miracles, signs, and wonders. The church in Acts didn't lack powerful displays of Holy Ghost power. May our New Testament ministry never experience a miracle deficiency.

Father, show us Your power and show us Your glory. Grant to us boldness and stretch forth Your hand to perform miracles, signs, and wonders, that the world would experience Your touch of love and marvel. Lord God, I want to see the works done in Acts be done in my life also. Give opportunity to step out in faith, that Your name would be glorified in all the earth. My praise is ever toward You. In Jesus' name, amen.

A Singular Message

> And I, brethren, when I came to you, did not come with excellence of speech or of wisdom declaring to you the testimony of God. For I determined not to know anything among you except Jesus Christ and Him crucified. (1 Corinthians 2:1–2 NKJV)

I recently had an friend in my office for a conversation about local influence and vision. With a smile on his face he said, "I only have one message. I don't have anything besides Jesus Christ and Him crucified." How refreshing! We aren't pouring out a 50 page theological thesis upon people. We are sharing the cross. May we never be corrupted from the simplicity of the gospel (see 2 Corinthians 11:3).

It's important that we never feel pressured to give the lost more than the simple gospel of grace. We can't add to or take away from the profound simplicity of Scripture. A compromised gospel is the foul offspring of a desire to please man more than God. The world's salvation doesn't require philosophy or deep earthly wisdom. It requires the knowledge of the death and resurrection of our King.

I remember telling a girl about the prayer of salvation and the simplicity of our gospel. She couldn't wrap her mind around how easy obtaining heaven could be. People are so used to jumping through hoops and dodging bullets to get what they want. In the Kingdom of God, we get what we want and go where we go through unmerited favor. The wages of sin is death but the gift of God is eternal life through Christ Jesus our Lord (Romans 6:23).

Invite the world into this free salvation. The message you carry is simple, yet perfect. Never make complicated the thing that God declares to be simple.

Father, now is the time to preach. Why wait another day? I desire to be fixed on You and the simplicity of Your wonderful gospel. May we set out to share Jesus Christ and Him crucified. Many are talking about Jesus but leaving out the cross. I shall share Jesus and Him crucified. May we never leave out the sacrifice of Your life. Thank You for imparting into me a message which I now impart into others. I pray this in Jesus' name, amen.

Everyday Anointing

...and I have filled him with the Spirit of God, with wisdom, with understanding, with knowledge and with all kinds of skills ... (Exodus 31:3 NIV)

He has filled them with skill to do all kinds of work as engravers, designers, embroiderers in blue, purple and scarlet yarn and fine linen, and weavers--all of them skilled workers and designers. (Exodus 35:35 NIV)

If you want to miss the anointing of God in your life, relegate the anointing to spiritual acts like preaching or prophesying. Like in the construction of the tabernacle, God wants to put His Spirit upon people for very natural, practical skills and abilities. Don't think that God is only interested in church services or revivals. The Lord wants to fill you with special kinds of skills and understanding so that the everyday work you do isn't done in your own might but in the creativity of the Holy Spirit.

When I first entered full time ministry, my job involved a lot of construction projects and facility maintenance in the church.

I learned much from men who were gifted by God in these areas. If we want to influence properly and effectively, we must find our unique anointing and learn to grow in it—whether it's architecture, accounting, communications, art, or business.

In 2 Chronicles, the Lord needed laborers with creative ability to renovate the house of God. "Then they entrusted it to the men appointed to supervise the work on the Lord's temple. These men paid the workers who repaired and restored the temple. They also gave money to the carpenters and builders to purchase dressed stone, and timber for joists and beams for the buildings that the kings of Judah had allowed to fall into ruin. The workers labored faithfully …" (2 Chronicles 34:10–12 NIV)

I believe the most critical statement of the verse is that they "labored faithfully." Discover the special kinds of talent that God has blessed you with and labor with faithfulness to the work God has cut out for you. As you operate in your practical anointing, your influence will be fulfilled in the very field God has called you to. May your work be a reflection of the excellence and brilliant nature of God Himself. Be a faithful laborer, not a fickle laborer. Work ethic isn't just a good quality—it's an influential testimony of the persistence of God in your life.

Father, I am made in Your very image. I want the creative work that I do from day to day to be a sermon to my peers. Your Word says that the work I set my hand to shall prosper. I honor You for prospering my work that Your name would be glorified through it. I understand that I have a unique anointing upon my life which I shall function in to see that people around me are saved, touched, and freed by the power of the gospel. Use all of me and use me frequently, O God. I desire this in Jesus' holy name, amen.

Your Sphere

> We, however, will not boast beyond measure, but within the limits of the sphere which God appointed us—a sphere which especially includes you. (2 Corinthians 10:13 NKJV)

God has appointed a specific sphere for our voice to be heard. The Bible is littered with emphasis on geographical locations. Don't discount the vitality of you being where you are. Within your God-given domain are people who are susceptible to the words coming out of your mouth.

When the Lord places us in a certain region, He is giving us the land. (see Joshua 1:3) What do we do with our land? We loose the will of God and bind the devices of Satan. (see Matthew 18:18) We drive out wickedness and introduce the order of the Lord.

In the Bible, God strictly and specifically gave Israel a directive to not stop fighting until every inhabitant was driven out of Canaan, yet we see that often times, Israel settled and allowed the enemy to occupy their God-given province. This became a thorn in the flesh of Israel. (see Numbers 33:55)

Too often we settle with a mixture of Christianity and compromise in our territory. We settle with results that don't cut it. Are there any unwelcomed inhabitants in your sphere of influence that need to be driven out?

Father, You've given me a sphere on the earth to touch, impact, and purge for Your name's sake. I make a draw on Your grace to drive out any and every inhabitant which doesn't belong—that the name of the Lord Jesus would run swiftly and be spread vastly in the place You've set before me. I pray this in the precious name of Jesus, amen.

Exceedingly Abundantly

> Now to Him who is able to do exceedingly abundantly above all that we ask or think, according to the power that works in us ... (Ephesians 3:20 NKJV)

Evangelism without power isn't biblical evangelism. Repeatedly, Paul would emphasize that his presentation was not in word only but in demonstration of power (see 1 Corinthians 2:4 and 1 Thessalonians 1:5). Jesus wants to showcase Himself in more ways than a Sunday morning service.

It's important that we push for the miracle and contend for manifestations of healing and deliverance. Too often, we preach to believe God for big things, that nothing is impossible, yet when we are faced with impossibilities, we have a whole lot of excuses and no power to show for it. I believe that God is willing to do more than what we are willing to believe Him for. If we say that He is big, we had better act like it.

In your job, on the streets, and in your homes, people are looking for more than a passport to heaven. They need a touch here and now—spirit, soul, and body. Thank God that He comes down to our neck of the woods and meets us where we are. Believe the Lord for big things. The healing Scriptures in the Holy Bible aren't to be a wish list for us but instead a covenant rite to see this act of love manifest.

Today, wherever you show up, remember to not only show up in speech but in demonstration. "For the kingdom of God is not a matter of talk but of power." (1 Corinthians 4:20 NIV)

Father, I am after a greater demonstration of You. Anyone can talk. I don't want just talk or speech, I want a display of Your covenant of health and wholeness. Bless and touch those whom I encounter today. I want to see them with Your eyes, O Lord. In Jesus' name I pray these things, amen.

Volume

Then he was told, 'Go, stand on the mountain at attention before God. God will pass by.' A hurricane wind ripped through the mountains and shattered the rocks before God, but God wasn't to be found in the wind; after the wind an earthquake, but God wasn't in the earthquake; and after the earthquake fire, but God wasn't in the fire; and after the fire a gentle and quiet whisper. (1 Kings 19:11–12 MSG)

Holy Spirit doesn't always talk loud. The whisper of God is a display of our closeness with God. We ought to fully cherish subtle and quiet leadings. It's expedient that we proclaim in public the whisper we hear in private. Your job isn't to be a container but a river. That means that the voice you hear must become the voice you share.

In order for you to speak for God, you must first hear from God. Someone once pointed out that God gave us 2 ears and only 1 mouth, meaning we should listen twice as much as we talk. As we lean into the heart of God in our devotion, He will speak and we will hear. Then what do we do? Peter made it clear in Acts: "For we cannot but speak the things which we have seen and heard." (Acts 4:20 NKJV)

Prophetic ministry is a means by which God is convicting the lost and edifying the church. Paul said to desire spiritual gifts, *especially the gift of prophecy.* (1 Corinthians 14:1) We are not a channel for the wrath of God on the earth, but a channel for the voice of God on the earth. Avail yourself to leaning into His voice and relaying His wonderful whispers to a people starving for a divine connection.

Father, I want to hear You. Give me a word for Your people, that I may have something to say in due season. I'm thirsty for influence and the world is thirsty for change. Let it come to pass as we press in, O Most High. I believe You for these things in the precious name of Jesus Christ, amen.

A Ready World

> …and after he brought them out, he said, 'Sirs, what must I do to be saved?' (Acts 16:30 NASB)

The prayer of this jailer is being echoed by the masses across the world today. The world is asking questions that only the church can answer. The world is presenting enigmas that only the children of God are able to solve. People are ready to be saved, but is the church ready to tell them how?

I was once in a hotel walking to my room and noticed an employee to my right. Holy Spirit stopped me in my tracks and quickened me to witness to him. I walked over and began to love on the guy, encouraging him. A couple more guys came into the area, so I shared with them, telling them who God is and who they were. I prayed over them and left. A night or two later at the hotel restaurant, one of the guys I shared with was serving our table. He said to me with little hesitation, "I'm ready to give my heart to God." Immediately, there on the job, he got born again.

God is dealing with the hearts of men. The Lord convicts and draws in humanity. I encourage you, plant seed and let God do the convicting. In evangelism, there is no such thing as bending someone's arm into salvation. Manipulation will never produce salvation. Be someone whose life alone gets people groaning for a faith walk. You won't be begging people to get saved. They will be asking you, "I am ready. What must I do?"

Father, if the world is ready to be saved, I am ready to give the invitation. No matter where I am, keep me quick, sharp, and on my toes—ready to give the Word of the Lord. I praise You for Your faithfulness to save. I pray all of this in Jesus' name, amen.

DAY 61

Get Out of the Way

> Do not think in your heart, after the Lord your God has cast them out before you, saying, 'Because of my righteousness the Lord has brought me in to possess this land' ... (Deuteronomy 9:4 NKJV)

You can't muscle a mountain to get it pushed into the sea. Only the word of faith will do that (see Mark 11:23). Life is less about us than we might understand. It's a mistake to think that ministry rises and falls with your ability to perform. If our performance was sufficient, we'd be preaching ourselves instead of the cross. We are only clay. Clay has no power until it meets the hands of the potter. All of our influence is done by Him and for Him; otherwise, it's futile.

As we remember that it's God who's doing it, it takes the pressure off of us. I distinctly remember the Lord speaking to me on this subject in a time of prayer. He said, "The only way that you would feel under pressure is if you're still the one running the show." You see, whether it's pulpit ministry or one-on-one interaction, we give God reign, thus alleviating our pressure because He takes responsibility for it. I'd rather trust in His anointing, not my intuition.

Be careful that you don't carry a weight that you were never meant to carry. Pass your pressure onto the One who can handle it. It's the Lord who fills your mouth with words and it's the Lord who backs those words with demonstration.

Father, I refuse to be crushed by the weight of ministry pressure. I'm not under any pressure to perform. It's You who works in me to do and to work, for Your good pleasure. All that I am is yielded clay. As a master potter, use me in the exploits that this day will present. In Jesus Christ's amazing name, amen.

The Blessing

> But without faith it is impossible to please Him, for he who comes to God must believe that He is, and that He is a rewarder of those who diligently seek Him. (Hebrews 11:6 NKJV)

A novice with zeal will get more done than an apathetic veteran. Passion seeks and saves that which is lost while apathy naps.

Not long after getting saved, I found myself walking the streets of my city with a friend at night, looking for folks to target with the love of God. One night, we approached a young man near a public pavilion. Upon talking with him, we found that he was homeless and lost. He pulled out a piece of drug paraphernalia and explained that just before we approached, he was planning to get high. Jesus knows how to intervene at the ideal time. That night, we ministered to him for probably 2 hours and brought him to church the next morning. In that service, he came to the altar to receive King Jesus. Within a week of this heart change, he was given a place to live, a job with income, and a group of

Christian co-workers to encourage him along the way. The Lord is faithful to follow up with those who call upon Him.

God had a storehouse of provision aimed at this young man, and his salvation triggered a release of the blessing. Our job as Christ-like influencers is to steer people into the direction of their promised reward. I've found that many are living in the wilderness and are completely content there. We don't have a destiny in the wilderness but a Promised Land.

I once visited a young man in jail who had previously been homeless. Without knowing why, I spoke to him in a strong way, "This homelessness thing has got to end." He responded, "Being homeless was the best time of my life." He went on to tell me about the miracles he saw every day in that state. "People would slow down in their car, roll down their window, and hand me a pizza as I walked down the street." I immediately responded, "When will you be the one driving the car, rolling down your window, and handing the pizza to the person in your position?"

See, the Lord meeting us in the wilderness daily to meet our needs is not motivation to stay there but motivation to cross over into our Promised Land. Never neglect the promise land because you're satisfied in the wilderness. Some refuse blessing because of pride or an unscriptural idea that blessing is bad. God is catching the attention of the world by the blessing that rests upon His church. Will you yield to the blessing? God is provoking the world to yearn for what you have.

Father, the Promised Land You have set before me is my destiny. It's a place of great impact. May the lost see it and yearn for it. I'll walk where You desire me to walk to see to it that the earth around me looks different after I pass by. Shake us and shape us by Your Spirit, O Lord. We aren't content with insufficient influence. We want it all, God. In Jesus' mighty name, amen.

DAY 63

The Real Fight

For we do not wrestle against flesh and blood, but against principalities, against powers, against the rulers of the darkness of this age, against spiritual hosts of wickedness in the heavenly places. (Ephesians 6:12 NKJV)

I don't believe that the devil is threatened by just any christian. I believe he is threatened by christians who have something to say. He is threatened by Christians who carry a sword in their hand and the high praises of God on their lips. God forbid we be Christians who don't threaten the works of darkness. Jesus was manifested to destroy these works. Why don't we do the same? The effect you have on the world depends on how willing you are to fight for it.

Pop culture is drawn to a good fight. People love battle stories. God planted His victory flag on the earth when He planted the cross at Calvary. The statement was gruesome and clear: people are worth fighting for. Never be quick to throw in the towel or give up on the folks that you are believing for.

"How can I give you up, O Ephraim? How can I surrender you, O Israel? How can I make you like Admah? How can I treat you like Zeboiim? My heart is turned over within Me, All My compassions are kindled." (Hosea 11:8 NASB)

If you find it easy to quit on a person, you might allow the Spirit of God to evaluate your love levels. The compassion of God makes it difficult to allow somebody to continue in paths of sin and self- destruction. Our challenge as influencers is to be diligent in remembering who our battle is against. I've watched people backslide and ricochet during the discipleship process, and the temptation is to grow angry and bitter toward the person. It's crucial that we bear in mind that demonic spirits and powers are at work behind the mishap. Otherwise, we will cast out the person and the devil continues on unnoticed.

Faith means getting your hands dirty. Interaction with the lost is taboo in some circles. Folks don't want the lost to taint their pretty Christian culture. They want to cast the lost out of their culture when the solution is casting the devil out of the lost. A Jesus loving church is the cure for the struggles of this age.

Today, be a cure. In your prayers and in your interaction, remember that the person before you isn't your enemy—Satan is. Mark out humanity for the love and salvation of our God through the One and only Jesus Christ.

Father, I recognize that contending for the salvation of the world is warfare. Since victory is already promised, fighting is made simple. Come and breathe Your sufficient grace upon Your church to fight the good fight of faith. I'm not okay with people going to perishing in their sins. I'm not okay with lives being destroyed. We need the move of Your Spirit. We need an outpouring. Let us target the works of darkness and see the works of God magnified in the earth. We trust You, Mighty God. I pray all of this in the wonderful name of Jesus of Nazareth, amen.

Perverted Priorities

> ...while we look not at the things which are seen, but at the things which are not seen; for the things which are seen are temporal, but the things which are not seen are eternal. (2 Corinthians 4:18 NASB)

The majority of people in our society believe in eternity, but how many of these people are living like it? More than once, I've met people who claim to genuinely believe that they will end up in separated from God for eternity. Why isn't this reality spurring them to change? Eternal plans have been replaced by earthly priorities.

When I was 21, I spoke to a man on the street about eternity. He seemed very apathetic and uninterested. In the middle of the conversation, he walked away from me and did a drug deal. When he turned around, his face was bright and he was well pleased. It's disappointing when your witnessing session gets interrupted by a drug deal. Talking about eternal truth did nothing for him while a carnal exchange made his day. He was uninterested in the things that mattered, yet captivated by the things that didn't. Our mountain is penetrating cultures like this with truth.

You might work with folks who will talk for hours about drugs, sex, and alcohol but won't spend a minute talking about life after death. We want to cause people to turn their attention to the things that matter. Often times, you will find that you care about someone's hereafter more than they care about their own. God put eternity into the heart of every human on the earth (Ecclesiastes 3:11). Whether they claim to believe it or not, mankind has an understanding that there is something more that lies beyond the confines of time. This gives us an upper hand when dealing with the issue of eternity. We are able to connect to an inherent conviction in the hearts of those we influence.

If you're in a room full of people and you begin to gaze at one particular area of the ceiling without ceasing, eventually everyone will begin to turn their heads to see where you're looking. People are interested in where you're focusing. If we live convicted lives with eyes on heaven, our contemporaries will switch their focus from temporal to eternal.

May our prayer be that our colleagues and families would approach us with questions like, "From where do you draw your strength? How have you found such peace?" When you have something good, people want to know where you got it. Today, be a living sign pointing to your Source and Savior.

Father, my heart is set upon You. You have captivated my focus. My attention is Yours. It's my desire that my friends and family would find themselves looking at what I look at—for I have set the Lord before me always. There isn't a moment that goes by in which You aren't my everything. Both here and hereafter, I am Yours and You are mine. Let this perspective be the perspective of many, dear Father. I pray these things in the holy name of Jesus, amen.

The Life of a Sower

> Now He who supplies seed to the sower and bread for food
> will supply and multiply your seed for sowing and increase
> the harvest of your righteousness … (2 Corinthians 9:10
> NASB)

God will entrust lots of seed to those who are willing to plant it.
When you thank Jesus for a breakthrough that happens at work
and your colleagues hear it, they know who gets credit in your
life—that's seed planted. When you call a distant friend on their
birthday—that's seed planted. When you intentionally rejoice
with someone who just received a promotion—that's seed planted.
It isn't complicated. It's Jesus.

In time, seeds yield a harvest. Live with hopeful expectation that
what you sow will grow. For about 2 years, I planted seed into
the life of a lady that I worked with in a secular job. I talked faith
with her and prayed for her a handful of times. I lived pure in a
way that contrasted with many of the employees at the company.
Lights cannot blend with darkness, they can only shine.

I was about to quit this particular job to move on to another, but before I left I wanted to invite this particularly lady to make a commitment to follow Jesus. It was the last time that she and I would work together and I considered the timing to be ideal. I prayed before going into the work shift and I heard the Spirit of God tell me, "She has unforgiveness in her heart." In the natural, she was a very sweet lady whom you would not peg to harbor bitterness—but God had spoken. I remembered the Scripture in Matthew 6:15, "But if you do not forgive others their sins, your Father will not forgive your sins." This is colossal statement. Our preaching ought to target the dangers of bitterness.

Just after clocking out in our final shift together, I began speaking with this lady. I gave her the invitation to receive Jesus and she was quite willing to accept this wonderful salvation. But before leading her in a prayer to confess Christ, I said, "I've got to ask, is there someone that you need to forgive?" Her countenance shifted and this sweet lady

became quite frustrated and bitter. "Yes, but I won't forgive her!" I interrupted, "But the Bible says ..." She cut me off and told me that she didn't care what the Bible said. This particular person had hurt her and her daughter seriously and she was refusing to let it go.

Holy Spirit was sniffing something out for sure. I didn't have all day to counsel and comfort. I quoted Matthew 6:15 to her as best as I could. As I shed light on the bitterness, she came to a place in which she was willing to forgive. I led her through a prayer of forgiveness and a prayer of salvation right then and there. Months later, I saw her and she told me that since that day, her life was given an "ease" that wasn't there before. It was simply seeds planted that ended in a harvest of forgiveness and salvation.

We are never short on opportunity to sow. We are, however, sometimes short on willingness to sow. The fields are ready and your work is cut out for you. Be inspired this day. Know that what you have put in the ground will not be forgotten. The Lord is monitoring and working on it. In due season, be quick and willing to give the ultimate invitation to come to the cross with repentant hearts.

Father, I will not let the seed in my hand go to waste. Show me how to be effective. Show us as the body of Christ how to make best use of what we have. May our potential influence be realized and the course of history altered because the church showed up strong. We love You mighty God. In Jesus' name, amen.

Condemnation Free Zone

> Therefore there is now no condemnation for those who are in Christ Jesus. (Romans 8:1 NASB)

Condemnation has an origin: Satan. Guilt is never God's doing. You might have a beautiful opportunity to speak up and pray for a person. You may be presented with an ideal chance to minister to a need. However, you find yourself with cold feet, nervous, backwards, or even apathetic and you let the opportunity slip. In that moment, we can either self-destruct or recoup. Satan wants to get in the ear of the believer with condemnation. Don't beat yourself up, build yourself up.

When you feel that you let an opportunity go, refuse to make it about yourself. Be quick to be inspired and encouraged to snatch the next opportunity that you have. Never allow yourself to be caught in a state of chronic self-evaluation. This will keep you out of action and out of influence. The devil would like to intimidate you and keep you in a fear of sharing your faith so that you remain silent. Then when you stay silent, he wants to condemn you for not speaking up.

I've spoken to people who have stepped out in faith and boldness to minister the Word of God, yet after they give the Word, they have thoughts such as this, "You did it all wrong! You shouldn't have said anything. You looked foolish, etc." Taking heed to these thoughts will produce nothing healthy in our lives. If a thought doesn't sound like Jesus, trash it. Shake off the guilt and press toward maximum influence through love.

When I first was saved and began my journey as a witness to my Lord, I often found myself pressured by the weight of condemnation. Without realizing it at the time, I would witness to folks out of a condemning impulse. In the realm of influence, you will be suboptimal if you're driven by guilt instead of being compelled by love.

Refuse the trap of condemnation, which will stifle your influence. Becoming self-critical happens through self-centeredness and our job is to deny self, that Christ might live, breathe, and move through us—free of guilt and full of love.

Father, I decline the invitation to be condemned about missed opportunity. This doesn't mean that I will be careless or lack urgency—but I certainly won't be kicked around for my failures. Let us never walk in guilty impulse, but rather true love and sincere hearts. Increase Your powerful touch to those who are saved and those who are on the outside. We want to see Your glory Father. Let it be done, I pray. In Jesus' name, amen.

DAY 67

A Heart for the Home

> ...but if a man does not know how to manage his own household, how will he take care of the church of God? (1 Timothy 3:5 NASB)

The greatest platform God has given us to make a difference is in our own homes. Paul plainly teaches that household management takes precedence over any public ministry. There is no congregation like the people you share life with everyday. It would be ludicrous to pursue influential ministry while neglecting relationships with spouses, parents, and children.

Be careful that you don't mix your evangelism with selfishness. It's improper for someone to try evangelizing their spouse for self-centered purposes. At that point, you become a Bible thumper rather than a people lover. The example you set will determine whether your family will desire or resent your faith walk.

The Lord designed the family unit to be just that, a unit. Some of the best influence that we can produce is dwelling in simple harmony with those we are closest to. Being the first to apologize or the first to reconcile is taking initiative that will catch the attention of people and cause them to see Christ in you—the hope of glory.

Jesus said, "Let the little children come to me, and do not hinder them …" (Matthew 19:14 NIV) It's never about forcing anyone to Jesus. If Jesus is presented for who He truly is, the little children will come. Our job is to simply encourage and never hinder it.

I grew up in a home where the peace of God was the centerpiece and the prize. My parents were sure to create an atmosphere of peace and any disruptions were not welcomed. We had a family friend growing up who would come over to our house to visit. While he was there, he would usually fall asleep on a chair within the hour. Why? Because he said that in our home, he felt peace. Rest comes easy in a home that is saturated in the tranquility of God.

How might you set an effective, godly tone within your home? Are you in love with every member of your family? Be the leaven in your home to see about the rise of everyone and everything around you.

Father, my home is Your home. Guard my family. Protect them under that shadow of Your wings. My first job is to represent Jesus within the walls of my home. I want to be consistently godly, whether I'm behind closed doors or in the public eye. Empower me for this I pray, Mighty God. Abba Father, I love You and thank You that my family is completely consecrated to You for Your divine purpose, according to Your manifold wisdom. I pray this in Jesus' awesome name, amen.

A Lesson in Leadership

> Furthermore, you shall select out of all the people able men who fear God, men of truth, those who hate dishonest gain; and you shall place these over them as leaders of thousands, of hundreds, of fifties and of tens. (Exodus 18:21 NASB)

A popular movie had come to our town and the theater was sure to sell out. My dad, brother, and I showed up before the theater opened to get tickets to the matinee. The parking lot filled with cars waiting for the doors to open.

With the doors locked, I decided we should get out of our cars and stand outside of the entrance to be the first ones in when the doors opened. When people saw us do this, the ice was broken and everyone got out of their cars and stood in line behind us. I looked at my little brother and said, "We broke the ice. That's a lesson in leadership." The line was long and the theater was packed; however, we got in the theater first and got to choose our seats. Why? Because we broke the ice.

People are looking for someone to go first. Humanity is hungry a model to follow. Our model and trailblazer is Christ Jesus. He came as a pioneer to demonstrate what a believer's life should entail. He didn't come to put on a show; He came to set an example. As we come under the leadership of Jesus, God entrusts us with leadership over people. The prerequisite to being assigned much is being faithful with little: " ...you have been faithful over a few things, I will make you ruler over many things ..." (Matthew 25:23 NKJV) Often times, feeling underutilized is a side effect of being faithful with the little.

Leaders have unique access into the life of their followers. There is a degree of influence found in leadership that isn't found elsewhere. Determine within yourself to break the ice and step out. You aren't waiting for someone to go first. The Lord your God has gone before you. He has blazed the trail. He has paved the way. Destiny isn't your reality until you pick up your feet and walk in it. The earth is waiting to see what you do so they can do what you do. May the display of your life be a shining representation of His.

Father, You've called us as pioneers. I'm not waiting upon man to make his move. I'm entering into the place and position of influence which You have ordained. I trust that as I lead, others will follow— yet they aren't following me, but You, Lord Jesus. I want to lead a life in which I am comfortable with people imitating me because I am first imitating You. Do what You please, Father. We love You. In Jesus' perfect name, amen.

The Great Intersection

> ...choose for yourselves today whom you will serve ...
> (Joshua 24:15 NIV)

Before the fall of man, the Bible records no dialogue between God and Adam. As a result, we aren't sure exactly what their relationship looked like; however, we do know that it was a Father/son relationship. In fact, Luke's genealogy records Adam as a "son of God" (Luke 3:38). When sin entered the picture, a dam was placed in the middle of intimacy with God for all mankind. Through insufficient sacrifice and works, man fought his way toward God with futile efforts. Then God planted His greatest weapon against darkness on the earth when He planted the cross at Calvary.

The very physical structure of the cross is an intersection. It's a place where horizontal met vertical. It's where sin met God's wrath. It's where sickness met justice. It's where we met love. "By this we know love, because He laid down His life for us ..." (1 John 3:16 NKJV) At this cross, the grace of God was dispensed on the earth, that humanity would partake. This grace to salvation redeemed mankind, not to a place in which we are servants or slaves—but sons of the Most High God. We are no longer bastard children. We have a Father. "For you are all sons of God through faith in Jesus Christ" (Galatians 3:26 NKJV)

The world that you're changing doesn't lack money. It doesn't lack people. It doesn't lack resources. It lacks a Father. Essentially, our efforts are toward welcoming the world into this fantastic adoption. It's the reason that we pray, "Our Father ..."

Ephesians 1:6 states that we have been "accepted in the Beloved." God accepting people has never been an issue. The church accepting people has. Give a warm welcome to all lost children. Pursue love and peace, and watch as the family grows.

"Pure and undefiled religion before God and the Father is this: to visit orphans and widows in their trouble, and to keep oneself unspotted from the world." (James 1:27 NKJV) Throughout the Scriptures, you will see God emphasizing ministry to both orphans and widows. Why? Because orphans and widows have something in common: there is a missing piece in their family structure. It is a missing piece that God Himself fills as a Father to the orphan and a Husband to the widow.

Father God is the greatest family member you have. Give Him away.

Father, You are my Father. Thanks for making me a family member. May my life lived produce brothers and sisters joining this heavenly adoption. Help me to speak to the fatherless about Your love. Enable me to present Jesus in a practical way to my contemporaries. My desire is that the family would grow. Let it be done, Father. I pray in Jesus' name, amen.

Viewing the Lost

Before I formed you in the womb I knew you, And before you were born I consecrated you ... (Jeremiah 1:5 NASB)

I once closed a sermon and was preparing to give an altar call to receive the Lord Jesus, per usual. In a moment of time, I had a vision. In the Spirit, I saw clearly a picture of an ultrasound. It left as quickly as it came. I didn't know what it meant. It came from left field—but I knew it was God. Then I heard the Holy Spirit speak. I opened my mouth and plainly said, "I just saw a picture of an ultrasound." God began to pour out the interpretation through my lips. "If you've ever had a child, you know that viewing an ultrasound is an exciting time. Even though the child isn't yet born, there is life, potential, and value there. You know that it will be your son or daughter." I continued, "When God looks at the lost, He sees an ultrasound. Even though the person is not yet born again, there is value, life, and potential there. God sees one who will be His son or daughter and He is excited about them!"

Prior to that encounter, I never knew that God was excited about the lost. We are so quick to point out where people are not. God draws excitement from the potential! Anyone can point out flaws in a piece of silver. Only someone with the right tools can refine it and draw out the goods. It's a mistake to criticize the lost. God-like results stem from seeing as God sees. Never grow accustomed to picking anyone apart. If you don't recognize one's potential, you won't be able to draw it out. You won't cultivate a property until you've seen that it's capable of bearing fruit.

Allow your normal perspective of the lost to be challenged. If you can't be challenged, you can't be trusted. The world doesn't need another critic. The world needs you and I to recognize the beautiful possibilities for their life by way of Jesus. Today, choose to envision a sinner apart from sin. Seeing someone for where they are takes common sense. Seeing someone for their potential takes uncommon faith.

Father, radically revolutionize the way in which I look at people. Those who are on the outside don't belong on the outside. I want to envision them as Your children and take that vision into a place of intercession. Move upon them, Lord. Pull out the potential of people. Draw out the value of humanity. Give us Your eyes, I pray in Jesus' name, amen.

Good God, Bad Devil

> The thief does not come except to steal, and to kill, and to destroy. I have come that they may have life, and that they may have it more abundantly. (John 10:10 NKJV)

This glorious passage in John's gospel may not be news to you, but it is to most of the world. Often times, the world lives contrary to God's Word, reaps painful consequences, and then begs the question, "Why is God letting all this happen to me?" John 10:10 clearly defines who is responsible for what. It's improper to blame God for the devil's doing. Many are blaming a blameless God and we must respond with an answer.

A seasoned Evangelist named Tim Grisham once sat down on an airplane and next to him sat a famous professional wrestler. When I say famous, I mean that they had wrestling dolls of this man for sale in Wal-Mart. Like any good evangelist, Tim leaned over and began to share the gospel. The man became quite angry and shut down Tim's attempt. He had suffered painful things as a child and held anger toward God for all of those things happening. In fact, exactly one week earlier, a different evangelist tried to witness to this man and he beat up the evangelist right there in the airport.

With rejection in his face, Tim waited for a moment and then pulled out his Bible, opening to John 10:10. He leaned over and showed the angry man this precious text and brought forth understanding that God isn't to blame. The man responded, "Why hasn't anyone ever showed me this before?" Tim was able to meet with him again for a follow up, and there this former NFL player and professional wrestler gave his life to the Lord Jesus Christ.

It all came from understanding being given that God is good. This must be a core value imbedded in the hearts and minds of every Christian influencer on the planet. Our goal isn't to develop an elaborate doctrine. We simply approach anything in life through the lens of this passage that the devil comes to harm but Jesus comes to save. Folks don't need to hear that God is harming them to teach them a lesson because that isn't true. God is a better teacher than that. Folks need to hear that we have a redemptive Savior who isn't to be blamed but is to be embraced in His fullness.

Many are pointing the finger at the One who has done no harm. Go into your realms of influence to clear up confusion with the truth of the gospel. Many don't know how to rightly divide the Word of God. You have to do it for them. Just as a small child, you must feed people until they can feed themselves.

Father, You are my prize and my aim. I believe that You are good. As a result, I can embrace You—free from fear. Send people to me, Holy

Spirit, who are in confusion about who God is. If I can declare to them who God is and who they are, everything will change. Abound Your love through our lives I pray, Father. In the holy name of Your Son Jesus, amen.

What's On Your Branches?

> For each tree is known by its own fruit. For men do not gather figs from thorns, nor do they pick grapes from a briar bush. (Luke 6:44 NASB)

You can debate theology, but you can't argue with fruit. The church has gotten good at winning debates at the cost of losing followers. Too often we would rather acknowledge disagreeable theology than recognize undeniable fruit. " ...filled with the fruit of righteousness that comes through Jesus Christ—to the glory and praise of God." (Philippians 1:11 NIV) Fruit is an arrow pointing to our Father. Good fruit upon your life is a trophy inscribed with God's name. Believe it or not, the world is looking for something ripe to be upon our lives.

As a rebellious high school student, I would sometimes spend time around people I had known to be christians. Perhaps I went to Sunday school with them or I knew that their parents were in the ministry. I would observe them and I could usually tell if they were still living for God or not. How could I tell? By the language coming out of their mouth. Our speech will either support the reality that we are Christians or contradict it. If the world sees that we have compromised our language, they'll assume we've compromised everything else.

Good fruit is the fabric of a good witness. The earth is groaning for an authentic taste of something they haven't experienced before. As sons and daughters, we have genuine fruit to share. The Spirit within you wants to display Himself outwardly through you.

What does this look like? "But the fruit of the Spirit is love, joy, peace, longsuffering, kindness, goodness, faithfulness, gentleness, self-control. Against such there is no law." (Galatians 5:22–23 NIV) Many of these qualities are foreign to the world. In fact, if you were to rattle off this list to some, they would consider it a fantasy. Their fantasy becomes reality when an active church grabs them by the hand, leading them to the One who satisfies all.

Father God, fill us with the fruits of righteousness. I desire that all good fruit would be seen in Your church. May there be no barrenness or lack. Fruitfulness shall be a testimony to the nations that the church of Jesus is planted in something real. Holy Spirit, amplify and maximize Your fruit in us. We are not a church of compromise. We are a church of holy fruit and influence. In Jesus' powerful name, amen.

The Ministry of Grace

...where sin increased, grace abounded all the more ...
(Romans 5:20 NASB)

For some, where sin abounds, judgment abounds much more. This is forsaking the model of God and embracing the way that seems right to a man—and it doesn't work. The world's sin should pull grace out of you, not frustration. In the ministry, we call some folks "EGR's" —extra grace required. Infants and toddlers require more time and focus than one who is mature and able to care for his or herself. My pastor always taught us that if we are going to err, err on the side of grace.

"Let no corrupt word proceed out of your mouth, but what is good for necessary edification, that it may impart grace to the hearers." (Ephesians 4:29 NKJV) If you want an impartation ministry, simply watch your mouth. Words proceeding from your mouth, if edifying, become grace proceeding from your mouth.

Paul exhorted for our speech to be "seasoned with salt and full of grace." (see Colossians 4:6) Grace is literally God's divine empowerment to do what's impossible on your own. It is unmerited. What do these words of edification look like? "I love you. You're valuable. I appreciate you. Thanks for doing what you do." These are simple words of affirmation that many people never even heard from their own parents; therefore, the impact can be massive when proceeding from your mouth!

As Christians, we have G-rated language in an R- rated world. As our speech is continually graceful, folks will walk away from a conversation with you with the ability to do something that they couldn't do before talking with you. "Thus saith the Lord" doesn't necessarily register with the lost. Simple phrases of love and life usually do. Call the waiter or waitress to your table. When they expect a request or a complaint, tell them, "I so appreciate what you're doing. You are amazing and Jesus loves you." Watch a smile develop on their face. You are to dispense the very grace and truth, which you've received.

Today, live as a continual dispenser of all that God is pouring out.

Father, if I can't give away what I have, I am ineffective in the work which You've set before me. I've got the living, eternal Word within me to dish out to the world. I declare that it's in me like fire and I cannot contain it, nor will I try. Lord, let nothing suppress the gospel ministry of grace in me. In Jesus' powerful name, amen.

Distinction

...A city that is set on a hill cannot be hidden. (Matthew 5:14 NKJV)

You are the city on a hill. You can't be hidden. God is interested in broadcasting who you are and what you have to a people who don't know Him. Romans 8:19 states, "For the creation waits in eager expectation for the children of God to be revealed." Creation isn't waiting for the revealing of a religious church. They've seen enough of that already. They are waiting for you and I to be revealed.

I believe businesses and companies are looking for a unique people. Status quo won't cut it. As children of God, we are in the world but not from the world (see John 17:16). We are easily the most distinct species on the planet. We should carry a mandate to take our distinct heavenly nature into our companies to see productivity and health maximized in our field.

If you're a confessing Christian, but you're lazy on the job, your witness is weak. I believe that Christians should be the best employees in the marketplace. Christians should have the most innovative ideas and cutting edge techniques. If one's faith were to be printed on a resume, Christianity should be a selling point—not a deterrent.

You and I can't change the world if we look just like it. The three Hebrew boys in the book of Daniel were completely distinct. Everyone in the territory bowed to a false god, yet these three remained standing. They had a posture that no one else did. As a result, they went through a trial that no one else went through, and by God's faithfulness, they had a glorious victory that no one else had. To this day, no one celebrates the stories of those who bowed to a false god. We celebrate the story of those who didn't. We celebrate the story of those who were distinct.

Carry your flavor into all the world. Your distinction is God-given. Allow yourself to stand out when most everyone fits in.

Father, being different is a beautiful testimony. You've called me and ordained me to be a difference maker in my company, in my home, and in all the world. I don't want to blend in, I want to stand out for Your glory. Reveal me as Your son or daughter, and I will reveal You as my Father. In Jesus' name, amen.

DAY 75

Caring for Eternity

...You must be born again ... (John 3:7NKJV)

My Associate Pastor once talked about how it would be a shame for someone to get healed and never get born again. I attended a power evangelism conference once and would listen to the people's testimonies as they got off of the street. Some would talk about word of knowledge flowing and folks getting healed—which I thank God for. But often times, I found myself hearing story after story of folks getting healed yet the salvation message was never extended to them.

I understand that our job isn't to hit the streets as a conversion machine, but it is important to at least extend an invitation to relationship with Jesus in some capacity. The last thing that I want to see is a generation that has a focus on miracles with no awareness of eternity. That isn't evangelism. The full gospel message of Christ is one that preaches present healing as well as eternal life and wholeness.

If angels in heaven lose it when one soul gets saved, sons and daughters of God ought to be able to lose it as well. I remember leading someone to relationship with Jesus in a parking lot once, and as the young man was walking away, I noticed a lady across the parking lot. I shouted to her, "Hey ma'am, that guy just got born again! Jesus is amazing!" She smiled and nodded. I rejoiced because changing eternity makes my day.

There is no life like eternal life. According to the Scriptures, eternal life is a must. Remember to make effort to connect the world with the One whom you've been connected with. We aren't chasing symptoms; we are dealing with the hearts of men. The only lasting miracle is eternal life through Christ Jesus our Lord.

Father, I pray that You would continually remind me to give invitation to receive Christ. I don't want to just display the power of God, I want to introduce all the earth to a heavenly Father. Altar calls should be normal in my life, O Lord. Draw all men unto Yourself. Thank You. In Jesus' name, amen.

Jesus the Standard Bearer

> ...the one who says he abides in Him ought himself to walk in the same manner as He walked. (1 John 2:6 NASB)

Jesus didn't come to put on a show; He came to set an example. We don't just admire His life, but we duplicate His life. The works of Christ are in reach. Jesus didn't commission His disciples with a downsized ministry. He actually commissioned them with the same ministry—a ministry that will, in fact, produce "greater works" (see John 14:12).

It's imperative that we not only preach the message He preached, but pray the prayers He prayed, and speak to the mountains which He spoke to. If Jesus is not our true model, we will begin to mimic our lives after something or someone who doesn't deserve it. Trying to find God's will in ministry outside of Christ's life is a formula for futile, worthless searching. The Bible describes us as co-laborers with God. It's impossible to co-labor if we are doing a different job than Him.

If Jesus healed the sick, then ministering to the sick is mandatory. If Jesus dispossessed demons, then the ministry of deliverance is mandatory. God forbid our ministry focus becomes different than His. If we're not watchful, we can drown power ministry in the midst of church activity and entertainment.

Since the beginning, seed has always reproduced after its own kind. Jesus has become the seed planted in the earth. He isn't reproducing inferior offspring, but offspring after His own kind to go about the same works.

Lord, send the sick and needy to me. Send those who are tormented and afflicted. I won't have an answer for them in my own self, but I have an answer in my God. Thank You for positioning me for the exact ministry which Jesus Himself carried out. Let me duplicate the gospels in the earth, Lord Jesus. Amen.

The Unending Supernatural

Rejoice always, pray continually, give thanks in all circumstances; for this is God's will for you in Christ Jesus. (1 Thessalonians 5:16–18 NIV)

When we see Him, we want to make Him seen. When we know Him, we want to make Him known. Our job isn't to collect encounters with God, but to give them away. Many folks live journeying from one encounter with God to the next, always seeking after grandiose experiences rather than faith-based relationship. We define miracles as "big miracles" and "small miracles," yet both are equally supernatural—both are equally God. If we are living for the next "big miracle" or the next "big move," we'll start to think God isn't as active when we are just seeing the "small stuff."

Whether someone gets out of a wheelchair or minor back pain is alleviated, both require God's complete involvement. If we only celebrate the big moments of influence and not the smaller ones, we've allowed our scale to compromise a life of thanksgiving. Paul was used by God to perform mighty signs and wonders among the people (see Romans 15:19). He was also used by God to collect sticks for a fire (see Acts 28:3). Whether we are used in the grandiose or used in the grind—it's God and we are thankful.

Buy into the reality that you're useful to God. You aren't living with a lack of influence. You're living above a lack of influence. Take note of the Holy Spirit's continual supernatural display in your life. Allow His faithful involvement in your life to spur you into faithful involvement in your neighbor's life.

Today, notice God. Emphasize His hand upon you and be encouraged to see that reproduced in someone else.

Father God, everything that You do is big. To You, nothing is impossible. Help me to daily take note of Your supernatural provision and never become apathetic toward miracles. I celebrate all that You are and ask for grace to pass this on to my generation, in the awesome name of Jesus I pray, amen.

The Chase

> Ask, and it will be given to you; seek, and you will find; knock, and it will be opened to you. (Matthew 7:7 NKJV)

The beat up and hopeless condition of society is to attract the generosity of the church. Lost souls won't always come to the church to seek answers. The church must seek lost souls to give an Answer. Jesus came to "seek and to save that which was lost." (Luke 19:10 NKJV) If our ministry involves no search or pursuit, we will bear less fruit than what's possible.

I have a ministry friend who displayed the pursuit with excellence. He worked a job which began at 9am. He didn't have a long drive to work, yet he would leave his residence at 6am. Why? He would drive his region searching for hitchhikers and people in need. He would give rides, take them in, feed them, help with money, and introduce folks to Jesus. Many struggle to wake up for the first 3 hours of the day, let alone search out a struggling humanity to offer an uncommon love.

In sales, cold calling can present more challenges than warm calling. In a warm call, the potential customer already has some familiarity with the product and may even be expecting the contact. With a cold call, you're breaking the ice and starting from scratch with someone. Seeking and saving involves plenty of cold calls. We are stretching ourselves and grasping for a humanity that may not expect any sort of contact. It's easier to pray, "Lord, send the lost to me" and do nothing than it is to seek out the lost and trust God to make the appointments.

"'I will rise now,' I said, 'And go about the city; In the streets and in the squares I will seek the one I love.' I sought him, but I did not find him. The watchmen who go about the city found me; I said, 'Have you seen the one I love?' Scarcely had I passed by them, When I found the one I love. I held him and would not let him go ..." (Song of Solomon 3:2–4 NKJV)

You and I will pursue what we value. Notice, the Shulamite bride refused to let go of the one whom she found. When we fight to obtain a thing, we won't allow it to be taken away with passivity. She pursued what she valued and preserved what she obtained.

Be exhorted today to hunt for the hurting and search for the lost. You cannot stay seated and change the world. Let's get up, go out, and mine for the gold that's in mankind today.

Father, because I seek You, I seek what You seek. I believe that You're searching out those who don't know You. By faith, I will step out and pursue people. When I walk into stores and restaurants, I want to care for the condition of the souls of the people. I want to be mindful of their lost state and ready to knock on the doors of hearts, prepared to display Christ. Thank You for Your heart in mine, O God. I pray in Jesus' name, amen.

Your Calling is Bigger than You

>...to open their eyes, in order to turn them from darkness to light, and from the power of Satan to God, that they may receive forgiveness of sins and an inheritance among those who are sanctified by faith in Me. (Acts 26:18 NKJV)

Sometimes we make the mistake of thinking that God chose us because we have it all together. A friend of mine once encouraged me with words I won't soon forget. "You have a destiny upon your life," he said. "Your destiny is bigger than you ... and it has to be that way, so you can't lean on yourself—you've got to lean on Him."

Attempting to fulfill God's calling without depending on God's grace will beat you up and wear you out. If you're doing a ministry that you can carry out in your own strength and ability with ease, it probably wasn't God who inspired the ministry. The Lord gives tasks to us which require His help to complete. A lone wolf mentality won't go far in the Kingdom. God likes it when our weaknesses are yielded to His perfect strength (see 2 Corinthians

12:9). In this place, influence is carried out on the earth through the perfect partnership between God and man.

Consider Noah, who was commissioned to build an ark for himself, his family, and all of the animals of the earth. I sometimes think to myself, building the ark would have been an easier task had Noah just built it for himself and his family. It would have been less labor, less materials, and less cost. Yet I believe he was commissioned to such greatness because his calling had to be bigger than him.

In Acts 26, Paul recounts his conversion to Christ. Jesus showed up, Saul's cage was rattled and he became blind for 3 days. Then Jesus said, "[I now send you] to open their eyes ..." Do you realize what happened? Jesus appears, blinds Saul, and then says, "Now go give people sight." Sometimes the Lord calls us to give things that we don't feel like we have. He calls us to give sight when we can't see. He calls us to forgive when it feels that we don't have an ounce of forgiveness in us. He calls us to encourage our family when we feel that we ourselves need encouragement. He calls us to minister to our co-workers when it feels that we are the ones needing ministry. When we are giving what we don't seem to have, we must borrow from His resources and not our own.

Today, you will fulfill a calling which is bigger than you but certainly isn't bigger than God. Lean on the anointing and grace of the Lord as you touch somebody with this glorious gospel.

Father, I thank You that Your call upon my life is bigger than me. I can't complete Your assignment on my own; therefore I look to You, my Help and my Strength. I desire to see revival among the people who are within my sphere of influence. I must be empowered by Your Spirit to see this come about. Lord, move through me this day in ways which are bigger than me. In Jesus' name, amen.

Doing the Impossible

...If you can believe, all things are possible to him who believes. (Mark 9:23 NKJV)

During my first trip to Jamaica, we visited an infirmary in the mountains of Montego Bay. An infirmary is simply a third world nursing home—a place in which people go to die. The conditions were poor and the people were seemingly hopeless.

As I sat on the edge of one man's bed, I began to share with him the gospel of healing and hope; both of us were nearly shedding tears. He took my Bible right out of my hand and said, "Wherever I open to, read from there." He opened the Bible and handed it back to me. I began to read the Scriptures and with each verse he would joyfully say, "Yes Lord! Yes Lord!" He knew that if he was hearing God's Word, he was hearing a good word.

Later that night, my friend and I were in the hotel restaurant reflecting on our time at the infirmary. God began to speak to me and I wept uncontrollably. I wept for this reason: I pictured a man who isn't necessarily well known. He isn't very popular. He doesn't come from an influential family. Yet He is walking by a sea called Galilee approaching several average, blue collar workers saying, "Follow Me." Over two thousand years later, I can travel to the four corners of the globe and find people who still know that Man's name—Jesus!

The reality of the worldwide spread of His name and His fame broke me and brought me to tears. If one man with 12 disciples could permanently mark the earth for the glory of God, what could you and I do considering we are empowered by that same Holy Spirit? We must break the "little old me mentality." Some folks consider changing the world to be too big of a task. I'm sure glad David didn't consider Goliath to be too big of a task.

Whether you come from a family of influence or not, God wants to move through you to change the world in an irreversible way. We know that nothing is impossible for God, but the Bible doesn't stop there. Nothing is impossible for YOU, if you believe! The only requirement for living a life free of impossibilities is believing.

Today, believe that you're anointed and equipped to make the world look different by giving away this amazing Jesus whom you have received. You're alive to make Him famous.

Father, I thank You that You have called me to be a world changer. In my own strength, my influence can do very little, but with Your supernatural empowerment, impossibilities become possibilities. I believe that You will move through me to share Your Word and will with a generation who does not know You. May my voice become one with Yours as I set out to show this world Jesus Christ. In Jesus' name, amen.

Building an Ark

> But Noah found grace in the eyes of the Lord. (Genesis 6:8 NKJV)

Realistically, many made fun of Noah's giant ark because they had never seen the slightest sign of flood waters. Yet surely they experienced regret when they were being drowned by flood waters—and only one man had a boat. Noah was commissioned to build a place of salvation. He preached for decades with no success, yet was not moved by a lack of results. He was moved by the commission of God.

You're the architect of a place of refuge for your generation. Paul said, " ...the wrath of God is coming upon the sons of disobedience ..." (Colossians 3:6). We often avoid these Scriptures in the name of being "under grace." However, this current dispensation of grace does not nullify the judgment to come. Our mandate is seeing a generation shifting from sons (or offspring) of disobedience to offspring of righteousness.

Every time that a sinner repents, they're welcomed onto a new covenant ark of salvation called the blood of Jesus—totally missing out on the wrath to come. Because we are in Him, we miss out on a whole lot of mess. One of God's beautiful attributes is His shelter. Psalms declares repeatedly that God is our shelter, our refuge.

As the last days draw near, truly safe places are growing scarce, yet the church has a sanctuary unlike any other. Live with a heart that is set on snatching humanity out of the fire. Welcome your world aboard the vessel of salvation that you've experience through the Son.

Father, I trust that I am building an ark. My life lived is preparing a place in which many can take shelter and find refuge. I've been saved from death, hades, and the grave. May I now return to those places to snatch folks out, just as I have been also. I pray this in Jesus' wonderful name, amen.

From Irritation to Invitation

> And he said to me, 'Son of man, I send you to the people of Israel, to nations of rebels, who have rebelled against me. They and their fathers have transgressed against me to this very day. The descendants also are impudent and stubborn: I send you to them, and you shall say to them, "Thus says the Lord God." (Ezekiel 2:3-4 ESV)

God didn't kickstart Ezekiel's ministry with an encouraging picture of the demographic he was called to. The folks lined up on the other side of Ezekiel's calling were rough, stubborn, and insolent. Would it be nice if we were sent to a warm-hearted people who welcomed us with a hug and hospitality? Oh yeah! But that isn't so.

Sometimes when we find ourselves working with people who are terrible rascals, we assume, by default, that the devil has introduced them into our lives. But what if there is a void in their life and you're the one who has something to fill it? After all, you and I are God's divine delivery system. You shouldn't be surprised when the Lord makes appointments between you and absolute sinners.

We have to shift from simply tolerating the lost to impacting the lost. Being easily irritated by people actually hinders our ability to influence those people. Our focus becomes their faults and failures instead of the faithfulness of God to sanctify and improve humanity. Whether it's family, co-workers, or any other group—the shortcomings of others are not a provocation for you to respond with irritation; it's an invitation for you to respond with the gospel.

In the sixth verse of Ezekiel 2, the Lord continued, "And you, son of man, be not afraid of them, nor be afraid of their words, though briers and thorns are with you and you sit on scorpions. Be not afraid of their words, nor be dismayed at their looks, for they are a rebellious house." (ESV) In order for the prophet of God to minister effectively, he had to hit the "off" switch on intimidation. Irritation and intimidation stifles influence.

Today, believe that people have been placed in your life on account of heaven's strategy. Some may be stubborn, but don't be dismayed. God is using you to give the world what you have.

Father, instead of complaining about the people in my life, I will pray for the people in my life. Touch them and bless them, I pray. Draw in their hearts and let them come to know You. If my attitude towards them ever becomes short-tempered or irritable, convict me and grace me to improve. I understand that I am heaven's delivery system—so use me, God, I pray. In Jesus' name, amen.

The Testimony of Stewardship

> The righteous care for the needs of their animals, but the kindest acts of the wicked are cruel. (Proverbs 12:10 NIV)

Righteousness isn't just seen in who you are, but it's seen in everything you touch. Even your animals, if cared for well, will carry a testimony of your righteousness. For example, I have a relative who raises Angus cattle. The cattle are well cared for, fed, and given plenty of land to graze and grow. He is also a born again, righteous man. If his livestock were malnourished, neglected, and abused, it would totally undermine the testimony of righteousness in his life.

I once heard about a certain landlord who rented properties. Most landlords will run credit checks in order to qualify the applicant. This landlord, however, didn't run credit checks. Instead, he would look at the inside of the potential tenant's car to see if the vehicle was well cared for. If the car was a mess and trashed, he would reject the application. He figured that if the car was trashed, his property would be trashed also.

How we handle what we've been given is determined by how much we value what we've been given. As Christians, we must value every good and perfect gift, big or small. Whether it's a household pet or a treasured relationship, our willingness to care will speak volumes to the world about our character. Excellence in all that we do is not to be forgotten or put off.

The 115th Psalm says that God has given us the earth. How we steward the earth will decide how we impact the people walking it. Today, operate with pristine quality in every facet of life. Watch as sound stewardship preaches a loud message to the world you live in that Jesus is excellent.

Father God, I'm thrilled to be in love with You. You have given me so much, and it would be a disgrace to trash what You have given. Help me to function in an excellent way, that the world would see the beauty and structure in the church and be moved to a place of repentance. May we, as the church, never be recognized for our sloppiness, but may we be recognized for our excellence. In Jesus' mighty name I pray, amen.

Your Story

> 'Return to your home, and declare how much God has done for you.' And he went away, proclaiming throughout the whole city how much Jesus had done for him. (Luke 8:39 ESV)

It's easy to share what Jesus did when you know that your life is a result of what He did. In Luke 8, Jesus instructed the man to share his story. Jesus didn't ask the man to become a biblical theologian and teach on the historical moves of God. He simply told the man to share his own story of the present work of God.

You have no better story than your story. I remember receiving a home-hitting prophetic word that the nations needed to hear *my* story. I'm fine with reiterating secondhand accounts of God's power, but I would much rather give a personal account of it. I tell people that as a preacher, if I'm called on to preach and don't have a message, I always have my story.

When asked about our faith, our mouth should never be empty. We are not short on personal accounts and testimonies of a faithful King actively involved in our day to day. Take some time praying and meditating on the mess that God has brought you out of. Ask the Lord to remind you continually of your mercy-riddled testimony. I find that when I reflect on my story, the Lord reminds me of details and scenarios that I had once forgotten. He shows me where He reached out to me and how He spoke to me.

Now that the blood of Christ Jesus has made us new, we don't run from the past; instead, we proclaim the God who conquered our past. Today, recall your story. Be ready to give a description of your salvation and the hand of God in your life. The most beautiful story you have is your own.

Father, I recognize that my story is a fountain of hope for people who are currently residing where I once was. Give me opportunity to tell the testimony that You have written for my life. Thank You for all that You are and all that You have given. I'm so in love with you. In Jesus' name, amen.

A Universal Void

Blessed are the poor in spirit, for theirs is the kingdom of heaven. (Matthew 5:3 ESV)

People need Jesus. You can't climb to a high enough social class or economic position to outrun your need of Him. We did door-to-door outreach and evangelism in our city with the youth group. We first went to a rough, impoverished neighborhood. Many were open and receptive to prayer and the gospel. A week later we entered an upscale, wealthy neighborhood. There we found that folks were not nearly as open to prayer and the gospel. They were short with us, quick to end the conversation, and many would avoid opening the door all together.

When we think we have it all, we stop receiving the things of God. Many believe that they are full and have their needs met apart from faith. They fail to recognize that it's the mercy of God that woke them up today. To influence those who see themselves as "full," we must point them to the One who gives the power to get wealth. It's God who is our rich Father and owns the entire world. One disaster could steal the riches from any man on the planet, leaving him with a broken kingdom which he built on his own.

Whether the person in front of you is rich or poor, they both have a spiritual poverty which can only be enriched by Jesus Himself. The Lord has leveled the playing field and declared to all that our own works are utterly insufficient. May these basic doctrines be restored in the heart of the church—pointing the rich and the poor alike to a sufficient Savior who fills the void that we couldn't fill on our own.

Father, I want to be sent to the world—every social class and every people group. All need You equally. Give me the words and the vocabulary to articulate truth to anyone I encounter. People are hurting, no matter what's in their bank account. I'd like to minister to the hurts and lead them to the cross, empowered by Your Spirit. In Jesus' name, amen.

Using What You've Got

> And when John had heard in prison about the works of Christ, he sent two of his disciples and said to Him, 'Are You the Coming One, or do we look for another?' (Matthew 11:2–3 NKJV)

When Jesus received this inquiry, His response was remarkable. He simply said, "Go and tell John the things which you hear and see: The blind see and the lame walk; the lepers are cleansed and the deaf hear; the dead are raised up and the poor have the gospel preached to them." (Matthew 11:4–5 NKJV)

This response which Jesus gave John was not news to John. He already knew that these things were happening. How do we know this? Verse 2 reveals, " ...when John had heard in prison about the works of Christ ..." John heard about the works of Christ, sent messengers to validate the facts with Jesus, and what is Jesus' response? Go tell John the works of Christ.

I believe Jesus is saying that we don't always need a new Word; we just need to believe the Word that we have already heard. A new and in-depth revelation isn't necessary for a good church service. Often I think that when we have heard certain principles repeatedly, we can easily exempt ourselves from conviction because we "already know it." You might have heard certain Scriptures a thousand times on Sunday, but the person you meet during the week hasn't heard it once—and you're the messenger.

Sermons cannot go from the pulpit, to the pews, and die before the closing prayer. Sermons must go from the pulpit, to the people, and to all the world. Our job isn't to go into all the world, keeping our faith to ourselves. Your relationship with God isn't just between you and Him. It's between you, Him, and everyone you encounter. Church gatherings are to inspire us in love to go out accomplishing good works. Let the Sunday service be your weapon throughout the week, destroying evil with good and changing your world one soul at a time.

Father, I no longer want to allow a Sunday sermon to be unfruitful in my life. What I receive in the house of God is meant to produce results outside the house of God. Thanks for equipping us in this way. In Jesus' mighty name, amen.

B.I.B.L.E., Yes That's the Book for Me

> All Scripture is given by inspiration of God, and is
> profitable for doctrine, for reproof, for correction, for
> instruction in righteousness … (2 Timothy 3:16 NKJV)

Our doctrine isn't being written, it has *been* written. Our ministry is Bible-based, without exception. As long as the Word of God is up in the air, our entire lives will be up in the air. The Scriptures are the rock which we return to, not a piece of clay to manipulate.

I remember leading an old friend from high school to the Lord in a local café. We later met at the same café for a time of learning and discipleship. He asked me where I found truth. He seemed slightly surprised when I relayed to him that the Bible was my source of absolute truth and nothing else. Our source material is found in Genesis to Revelation. Self-help won't take folks far, because self-help reduces you to your own resources and strength. God-help opens the supply of heaven to our situation.

Some folks claim to be Christians yet say, "I only believe parts of the Bible. Some of the stories are farfetched." The Bible is only farfetched to a carnal mind. The famous song declares, "Jesus loves me this I know …" How do I know? The song continues, " …for the Bible tells me so." If it's found in the Bible, it's good enough for me. The devil would like to talk us out of the promises of Scriptures and give us every reason why God's promises are not for us. God gave us one reason to prove that they are for us—His Son on a cross.

The truth we need to change the world is found in the pages of the Holy Bible. Use Scripture in dialog with others. You don't have to quote chapter and verse or recite passages in KJV, but certainly include the Word. For example, tell your waiter or waitress, "I want you to know that I believe the person serving the table is greater than the ones sitting at the table—and I just want to say thank you." That person may have no idea that you're quoting Jesus in Luke 22, but it's a point of entrance for God's Word in the life of another.

Today, be quick to return to the strength and life of the written Word. The Bible is your balance, keeping your witness sharp and full of truth.

Father God, Your Word is vital to my life and the lives of others. I don't want to memorize Scripture for the sake of memory. I want to learn Your Word for the sake of spilling it on the world around me. In Jesus' holy name, amen.

Built to Last

> One of those days Jesus went out to a mountainside to
> pray, and spent the night praying to God. (Luke 6:12 NIV)

God is strategic about influence. He wants to send us to folks we
can influence, without our integrity being violated in the process.
I see folks come out of a life of sin and get steady in church for a
short season. Then they feel that they can go back to old friends
and lead them in a grand revival back to church, but typically, they
return to old patterns instead of instituting new ones. Without
having integrity like steel, it's easy to be pulled down by sinful
scenarios instead of bringing life to sinful scenarios. I am all for
going back to old friends to introduce the gospel; however, you're
going back to stand out—not blend in.

"Do not be misled: 'Bad company corrupts good character." (1
Corinthians 15:33 NIV) When presented with this truth, people
respond, "But Jesus ate with sinners." While it's true that Jesus ate
with sinners, He also had all night prayer meetings to perfectly
align Himself with the Father. Why? I believe it was so that when
He went out to spend time with sinners, He could influence the

lost without participating in the lifestyle. Our purity cannot be violated in the name of "eating with sinners." If we are willing to eat with sinners, let's also be willing to pay the price in prayer ahead of time.

Our job is going into all the world. We can only pierce society effectively if we are introducing purity, not letting ours be defiled. Be the difference. Display your distinction. Live salty.

Father, I want to be able to go into the dark places of our world and hang out with the wretched and the lost. They need the influence that the church can offer. In that place, give us strength to influence them without being influenced by them. Thank You that Christians across the world would no longer participate in sin but lead their neighbors out of it. In Jesus' powerful name, amen.

Pursuing the "Yes"

> He said: 'Son of man, I am sending you to the Israelites,
> to a rebellious nation ... (Ezekiel 2:3 NKJV)

The Lord's assignment to Ezekiel wasn't a fun summer mission
trip. He was sent to an adamant people who didn't want change.
Interestingly enough, God didn't even guarantee their repentance.
Yet He still sent His prophet. Why? Because their potential to
reject a message doesn't keep the message from being sent.

Many grow discouraged when they see a lack of change in
those who hear the gospel. They grow weary at the shortage
of repentance in the crowd at hand. However, we should never
allow somebody's "no" to keep us from pursuing somebody else's
"yes." Jesus taught this by saying, if you're rejected, just kick
the dust of the city off of your feet and move on (see Matthew
10:14). Scripturally speaking, dust represents the natural man,
the flesh, and even death. "For dust you are, And to dust you
shall return." (Genesis 3:19 NKJV) When you kick the dust off
of your feet, you're literally making a statement that folks might
have rejected the giver of life, but you won't allow their state of

death to cling to you—so you're kicking it off and continuing on assignment.

We are not out collecting numbers, but we are gathering disciples. Our mission isn't to gain new notches on our ministry belt. Our mission is to love the one in front of us, permanently and unconditionally. Some won't receive your message, but rest in the comfort that they will indeed know that you were sent from God (Ezekiel 2:5). They could say "no" to what you present, but they can't deny that you are indeed a mouthpiece for the Most High.

Father, as Ezekiel was sent to the roughest, may we be sent to the roughest. Let love break stony hearts and let truth puncture the deepest stubbornness. It's Your goodness that leads men to repentance and Your goodness we shall display, in Jesus' wonderful name I pray, amen.

Found by God

> I revealed myself to those who did not ask for me; I was found by those who did not seek me. To a nation that did not call on my name, I said, 'Here am I, here am I.' (Isaiah 65:1 NIV)

In Scriptures and in our world today, there are certain regions that are under a heavier demonic influence than others. Some areas are quick to disregard a preacher and slow to repent, while others are quick to embrace the good news and quick to change their way. Many consider various areas to be spiritually cold and closed off to the church. At the end of the day, it would be good to ask ourselves, is God still bigger? This question can sober us and give us a boost to penetrate even the coldest areas with an irresistible love.

Many consider San Francisco to be a spiritual wasteland. I was once in San Francisco standing outside of my hotel, and a large man approached me asking for a cigarette. I didn't have a cigarette to give him. However, I did have Jesus to give him. It's always fun when you're fishing and the fish jump in your boat. As we talked,

I found out that this man had been saved years earlier but had no strength in his Christian life or in his prayer life.

I don't know of a better enhancement to the Christian life than the baptism in the Holy Ghost with the evidence of speaking in other tongues—so I began to teach him about it. Many are offended by tongues, yet speaking in tongues is more scriptural than a lot of church activity nowadays. It isn't a gift that we keep to ourselves, but it's a gift we should lead the church into.

I had this man pray for the Holy Ghost. If you ask the Father for bread, He won't give you a stone; if you ask for a fish, He won't give you a serpent (see Luke 11:12). This man asked for the Holy Spirit, and he got what he asked for. He began speaking in other tongues and worshipping the Lord Jesus right on the street in California. He approached me asking for a cigarette but walked away ten minutes later with the Holy Ghost.

God is showing Himself to people who aren't even searching. Why? Because He is still pursuing. Lay hold of the simple opportunities with strangers who cross your path—it might just be a God ordained appointment. The church isn't to be intimidated by spiritually cold places. We don't react to the environment, we determine the environment.

Father, let me never pass up the appointments You've set up for me. Connect me with those who need salvation, healing, and the baptism in the Holy Spirit. Enable me to pursue as You pursue and be available as You are available. In the name of the Lord Jesus Christ, amen.

Hit the Switch

> For I am already being poured out like a drink offering, and the time for my departure is near. (2 Timothy 4:6 NIV)

In the midst of the comfort of getting our needs met and be cared for by God, we can't lose sight of the rugged, unusual, sold out life that we are called to. I love prosperity—I think it would be false humility to say otherwise. However, it's a sin to replace seeking the Kingdom with seeking prosperity instead. A Christian life isn't merely collecting what we can get. It is also giving all that we obtain. If our import is not followed by export, we're missing half the battle.

Twice Paul referred to himself as a drink offering. It literally means that he was being exhausted in every way—nothing left in the cup. All that is within must come out. Many have gotten good at hearing the Word. Some have gotten sharp at doing the Word. Few have gotten comfortable sharing the Word. Sharing is not optional; it's a requirement.

Most genuine Christians admire true passion and want it for themselves. Yet many don't understand the price that one pays to live in it. Walking with Jesus has never been casual. It's always been radical. We don't simply collect encounters with God, but we give them away. Count the cost of a radically influential lifestyle. You'll find at the end of the calculation that it's always well worth it. God doesn't forget one ounce of sacrifice an individual makes for the gospel's sake.

Today, for the sake of the world, be the cup in the hand of God which He can pour out on the earth around you.

Father, I've already decided to be a living sacrifice. I'm not asking for a normal life. I'm asking for a Christ-like life. Mold us into radical influencers that fulfill a destiny that's bigger than us. I pray these things in Jesus' name, amen.

Jesus and Joy

> You love justice and hate evil. Therefore, O God, your
> God has anointed you, pouring out the oil of joy on you
> more than on anyone else. (Psalm 45:7 NLT)

I believe that a Christian life looks like smiles and laughter. When
I see paintings of Jesus portrayed with laughter, I'm soothed with
the reminder that He walked in a greater measure of joy than any
jokester in His time. I genuinely believe that the Lord wants to
increase the anointing of joy upon His church. Your joy might
just provoke the world to jealousy. Your laughter might just cause
your peers to want what you've got.

Wearing a smile is public testimony displayed on your countenance
that God is the source of your joy and nothing can steal it. Far
too many Christians look like the image of frustration rather than
the image of God. A bad attitude is a bad witness. When you
encounter people, they shouldn't feel like they're inconveniencing
you. If you're running out of patience with a person, it's awfully
difficult to love them into an encounter with Jesus. The church

must die to day-to-day headaches and come alive to the day-to-day influence written in our destiny.

It would be a shame to have a remarkable anointing in a public setting but a terrible attitude in a private setting. The world is trying to read who you are, and sometimes the only headline they see is the countenance you carry. May our lives be a joyous billboard pointing all to the One whom we love—Jesus.

Father, Your joy is my strength. I surrender my attitude to You. I lay down my rights to carry a sad countenance. I want to wear a smile in suffering and in celebration. Draw all men unto Yourself through our lives Lord, in Jesus' name, amen.

Lucky Duck

> I will remember the works of the LORD: surely I will remember thy wonders of old. (Psalm 77:11 KJV)

When people come across a servant of the Most High, like yourself, they tend to remember it. God has a way of lodging Himself into our memory. A simple phone call or word of encouragement might be quickly forgotten by the one who gave it. But that simple act of love is often never forgotten by the one who received it.

While doing ministry at a prison in northwest Indiana, I heard a unique true story with significant spiritual application and value. There was a flock of ducklings on the prison ground one day milling around. A hawk decided to swoop down and snag a young duckling for lunch. As the hawk flew away, its talons lost grip and dropped the prey. The duckling flew to the ground and smacked the sidewalk with force. Some inmates simply kicked it off of the sidewalk and into the grass—leaving it for dead.

Upon seeing this, one particular inmate decided that he would care for the duck and nurse it back to health. He began the process of caring for the bird and fittingly named it Lucky. Eventually, he was able to release the duck back into the flock.

Some time later, this inmate stood next to a prison volunteer as they looked out at a massive flock of ducks. The inmate said, "Watch this." He began calling out to the birds, "Lucky! Lucky!" Sure enough, out of the midst of this massive flock of birds, little Lucky Duck came limping back to the one who cared for it.

The moral of the story is simple: people remember those who invested in them when they were at their worst. Multitudes of people have been unwanted and left for dead, and the church is now living in prime time to act! As we do, the investment won't be forgotten. Humanity will remember the church that acted, not the church that slept. Let's arise and see to it that we assist in transferring people from the worst of the worst to the best of the best, through our King Jesus.

Father, I believe that when You call my name, I hear You. May the entire earth hear their name called, as well. Show us our opportunities to pick up a dying people and nurse them to health through Your Word and Your Spirit. In Jesus' name, amen.

Natural Ministry

> But whoever has the world's goods, and sees his brother in need and closes his heart against him, how does the love of God abide in him? (1 John 3:17 NASB)

Giving "spiritual" answers to natural problems caused John to question the love of God in a person. Spirituality is never to be a cop out for solving natural, physical issues. Feeding the hungry, clothing the naked, and caring for the poor are not just mentioned in Scripture but emphasized in Scripture. Providing a meal for a person can sometimes move them to Jesus in ways that a five point sermon wouldn't.

Meeting the natural needs of an individual ought to be an entry point to meeting the spiritual needs of that person. I remember praying once before leaving my home. I prayed specifically for the opportunity to give a coat away. That night, the appointment was made as I noticed a man standing outside with only a t-shirt on in the northern Indiana cold as snow fell to the ground. After I approached and gave him the coat, I was able to share this wonderful salvation message. He received Christ Jesus that night and never forgot it. After that night, he referred to me as "the coat man." Giving a coat was a simple act that opened the door to unforgettable, irreversible ministry impact on young man's life.

If we aren't careful, we'll forget that having our needs met is a given in Christ. Our good Father is sure to provide, thus our needs aren't our fixation. We've got to gaze into the eyes of a hurting world and jump at the chance to meet them in their lack. Our prayers cannot solely consist of petition to God for our needs to be supplied. Our needs are already supplied according to the written promise in Philippians 4:19. Our prayers must be geared toward petitioning heaven to invade the lives of those who can't access it themselves.

Even our fasting must not be self-centered. The Lord spoke to this in Isaiah: "Is it not to divide your bread with the hungry And bring the homeless poor into the house; When you see the naked, to cover him; And not to hide yourself from your own flesh?" (Isaiah 58:7 NASB)

Today, purpose in your heart to supply for those who are experiencing a shortage. We shouldn't just notice needs but meet needs. Be a conduit for heaven's resources to provide for your near ones.

Father, I open myself to being a minister of the spiritual and a minister of the physical. Help me to spot opportunity to feed the hungry and take in the oppressed. Give us wisdom as we search out the needy. Lord, I know that the goal of the gospel is that we transition from total lack to lacking nothing. May this message continually be on our lips, O Lord. I pray these things in Jesus' mighty name, amen.

Do it Now

...but exhort one another daily, while it is called 'Today,' lest any of you be hardened through the deceitfulness of sin. (Hebrews 3:13 NKJV)

Christians all over live with compromise and total lack of surrender, but comfort themselves by believing they'll simply repent right before death and secure their spot in glory. I used to embrace this concept when I should have run from it. It's a sick wisdom devised by Satan himself. He knows that if he can destroy a man, he can destroy a plan. If he can crush a person, he can cut them off from changing their world. Our job is never to delay our destiny but step into it right away. Procrastination isn't just a character flaw, it's sin. Influence is not one day. Influence is today!

The Lord Jesus has gifted us individually and uniquely to see to it that He is lifted up on the earth. If you have a gift in your life, you're obligated to use it for the One who gave it to you. When your gifts are complemented by men, let the praise pass over you—God wants to inhale the glory for it.

If you sing, change the world with your voice. If you dance, change the world with your expression. If you write, change the world with your books. If you paint, change the world with your art. If you run a company, change the world with your business. It has never been complicated. It's starting where you are, with what you have.

Consecrate your gifting to Christ and allow Him to anoint and move through every single talent you have for His glory and purpose.

Father, any and all gifting that I possess is just that—gifting. You gave it and I shall use it for Your purposes. Empower us to start where we are, Lord. I pray that all over the earth, men and women would rise up and roar with influence in whichever field You've placed them in. We aren't in survival mode barely getting by. We are thriving with the purpose of God prevailing every single day. In Jesus' name, amen.

The First Step

'Come,' he said. Then Peter got down out of the boat, walked on the water and came toward Jesus. (Matthew 14:29 NIV)

For many, breaking the ice and walking outside of comfortable parameters is tricky business. The initial step is sometimes the scariest. As I watch folks street witness for the first time, they are often overcome with hesitation and doubt. What do I say? Who do I talk to? What if they reject me?

Faith is able to launch without knowing the details. God's idea is that we step out and He fills our mouth with His Word (see Psalm 81:10). We usually want a script ahead of time, but the Kingdom thinks differently. The Kingdom likes risk.

David stepped out in risk as he came against an enemy of God. He had experienced triumph over the lion and the bear, but was now encountering his first public fight against the giant. Interestingly enough, Goliath only represented .014% of the enemies whom David would slay. After Goliath, David still had an unfulfilled hit list of 7,000 more men to kill (see 1 Chronicles 19:18). But what are 7,000 mere men when you have the head of a giant in your hand? It seems that we all have that one victory that makes the other battles look laughable.

Sharing your faith is a step of faith. Break the initial ice and experience the brilliant reward. As we overcome the giant of initial hesitation, I believe God has thousands of additional encounters lined up. Our work is not done with Goliath ... It's only getting started.

Father, I bind hesitation of any kind in my life. I fully believe that when I say yes to being Your mouthpiece, You say yes to providing the word. Come and speak through us as we encounter humanity day in and day out. Thank You for these things, O Lord. In the mighty name of Jesus, amen.

A Die Hard Message

> In fact, everyone who wants to live a godly life in Christ
> Jesus will be persecuted ... (2 Timothy 3:12 NIV)

If we allow people to break us, we'll depend on people to build
us back up. We can't afford to give people a place in our lives that
only God has paid for. Persecution isn't a possibility; it's a promise.
Those who are killed for their faith are the ones who are vocal
about their faith. The threat of "meeting your Maker" isn't a scary
thought if you've already met Him.

The devil's playbook contains nothing that can defeat the church
of the Lord Jesus. Our message isn't a philosophy or a theory;
it's an eternal truth that will never rust or fade. As persecution
increases, martyrdom will increase in the church. This isn't just
about being willing to share our faith. It's about being willing to
die for our faith.

Influence doesn't mean we promote ourselves. It means we deny
ourselves. Fearfulness denies Christ when the pressure is on. Christ
denied fearfulness when the pressure was on. His model works

better. We have a golden opportunity to display an authentic Jesus in the midst of opposition and persecution.

Today, settle within yourself to stand by the of God—even unto death. We would rather die than reject this Jesus who set us free. There is nothing wishy-washy about the life of a Christian. It's an extreme life cut out for an extraordinary people.

Father, I'm sold out for You. There is none upon the earth that I desire before You. Lord, we are not loving our own lives unto death. We will stand by the gospel, doubtless in the midst of any and all persecution. Thank You for Your dependability and faithfulness. We love You, God. In Jesus' precious name, amen.

Ministry from Sonship

'My son,' the father said, 'you are always with me, and everything I have is yours. (Luke 15:31 NIV)

You're most effective in ministering when you aren't merely fulfilling a task but are instead loving people. Things done out of "ministry obligation" are tainted with an impersonal tone. Things done out of generosity of the heart are anointed with unmistakable sincerity. Our relationship with God is not a "working relationship." It is a Father/son relationship. Slaves earn wages, but sons receive inheritance.

Touching the world with the gospel by no means earns us favor with God. We have already stepped into fully grown, fully developed favor with God through His Son Jesus. Touching the world is simply the result of a secret place connection with the Father. I remember the Lord once speaking to me in prayer, "Nick, I love you. Not for what you can do for me, but for who you are to me." It marked me in an eternal way.

People are valuable in the sight of God. As we set out to change the world, we aren't looking at potential converts. We are looking at potential sons and daughters. The world needs to hear from the church that they are valued. Value is not determined by a church membership or a religious affiliation. Value is determined by the price paid at Calvary. I've watched people get born again in parking lots simply by approaching with the question, "Do you realize how valuable you are?"

Today, let it be your honor and privilege to impact the sphere you live in. Don't be weighed down by religious duty, but be alleviated by amazing grace. People who have lost sight of their value are waiting for you to tell them the truth about who they are and why they are.

Father, I'm so thrilled to call You my Father. Everything I do in ministry must be done out of a life-filled Father/son connection. May I go out today and every day with a mandate to grow the family. In Jesus' awesome name, amen.

Making Your Money Influence

> May God be gracious to us and bless us and make his face shine on us - so that your ways may be known on earth, your salvation among all nations. (Psalm 67:1–2 NIV)

It's God who gives us the power to get wealth and it's also God who gives us the power to give wealth. Money isn't something that we idolize; it's something we steward. Prosperity is mandatory for establishing covenant on the earth (see Deuteronomy 8:18). The furtherance of the gospel is not a cheap venture and it must be supported by Christians who are able to handle wealth. Sometimes obedience means writing a check.

The 28th chapter of Deuteronomy outlines several curses of the law which come upon those who stray from the rules. By God's grace, we have been redeemed from the curse of the law by faith in the Son. (see Galatians 3:13) Included in the curse was sickness and poverty. Through strange tradition and lies, many have taken a "vow of poverty" in hopes of putting themselves on a higher level of spirituality. Poverty does not increase spirituality; it actually stifles it. Poverty is not a blessing—it's a curse. If you've ever taken the gospel overseas or been a part of leading mission trips of any kind, you know that it takes money, and plenty of it to work effectively.

I confidently believe that the Lord is raising up a generation of Christians in the marketplace who will cause the demonic to tremble because the wealth of the wicked is being deposited into the account of the righteous. The kingdom of darkness experiences casualties when you're blessed. The checks that you write could put demons to flight. Prosperity isn't a shallow doctrine about getting our ducks in a row and driving the best cars. It's a God ordained principle to invest in the best kingdom.

Are you someone whom God can channel resources through? Be a vessel through whom God can supply the work of the Kingdom on the earth. Never allow anyone to talk you out of prosperity. Being prosperous is the continual state of God. It's a continual state of influence.

Father, as the Psalm declares, be gracious to us and bless us, with the intent that Your way is made known and Your salvation is declared among the nations. Use us to steward Your wealth properly, to see to it that end time revival is never short on monetary resources. Thank You for this route of influence being maximized in the body of Christ. In Jesus' mighty name, amen.

Always On

I have set the Lord always before me ... (Psalm 16:8)

Your influence shouldn't have an "off switch." A lover doesn't stop loving when trouble shows up. An influencer doesn't shut down when the going gets tough. Jesus said, "Let your light so shine." He never mentioned turning it off. Don't allow personal problems to steal from your ministry. There is a lie which would say that you must have all of your ducks in a row before you can be effective. No one has ever been perfect, nor will anyone ever be perfect, yet God has always used people and He always will.

When I was 21, I was driving home from being out of town. It was a frigid November night. Just past 2 in the morning, I noticed a deer standing in the middle of my lane. I was moving at about 85 miles per hour and had no time to stop. I unwisely swerved and lost control of my car. Just before hitting a tree I said, "God, help me!" —I was beyond helping myself.

I hit the tree hard. Greater pain than I'd ever felt filled my back and midsection. I wiggled my toes, making sure I wasn't paralyzed.

As I moved my left leg, I felt bones shifting and popping in my lower back. It was cold, late, rural, and my phone was dead. In that moment, I heard a nasty voice say, "How real is your God now?" I laughed and rejoiced in the face of accusation and then heard the voice of God say, "I am with you." I had perfect peace which transcended my understanding.

Somehow I managed to exit the car through the passenger door. As I stood and limped to the road, it felt as though a hot soldering iron was being stuck into my back. I stood by the side of the road waiting for a car to come. I saw headlights and began to wave my arms. To my surprise, the car kept driving right past me. At that point, I could no longer stand. I laid down next to the road and waited for another. A second car approached. I waved my arms. The car kept driving, to my dismay. I waited again. The third car came. The third car went. The 25 degree weather was getting to me, and lying on a cold road didn't help.

A fourth car approached. I tried getting their attention, but again they kept driving.

Desperate, I decided to drag myself to the middle of the road. As I lay in the road, a fifth car came. I quickly scooted to the opposite lane and raised my hands. Just after the car passed me, I saw brake lights. Out came a very concerned 21 year old. I told him, "I crashed from swerving to miss a deer. I think my leg or my back is broken and I need you to call 911, my phone is dead." He went into his car and called. He came out and told me that 2 units were on their way.

I then began a conversation with him. I asked him, "Hey man, do you know Jesus?" It's a simple question, but one that is certainly worth asking our neighbors. He replied, "I knew Jesus, but I've gone astray and backslidden." I said, "Well, come over here man, let's fix that." He knelt down, grabbed my hand, and recommitted himself to Jesus in the middle of the road.

Hearts become open in crisis situations. They can make for ideal times to demonstrate the King and watch the world respond. After that, he covered me with a coat as my whole body trembled from the cold. Typically, a 21 year old lying in the road in the middle of the night with a crashed car has had some alcohol. The cops and EMT's arrived asking, "Have you been drinking tonight?" I said, "No sir, I'm a preacher." They loaded me up and took me to the hospital. I suffered 5 breaks in my pelvis. The doctor said that I wouldn't walk for 8–12 weeks. I was using a walker in about 2. God healed me with divine completeness.

In a moment of weakness, the devil wanted to capitalize, but God wanted to show Himself strong. The Lord brought salvation out of a mess. "And we know that in all things God works for the good of those who love him, who have been called according to his purpose." (Romans 8:28 NIV)

Father, opportunity is everywhere. Enable me to capitalize in every situation. I see that the fish are biting. People are ready and willing. Make me ready and willing also. Pour out a great measure of anointing, more than we've experienced. We say 'yes' to anything that You will, Father God. In the holy name of Your Son Jesus, amen.

DAY 101

The Pilate Generation

> …having examined Him in your presence, I have found no fault in this Man … (Luke 23:14 NKJV)

At the trial of Christ, Pilate found no fault in Jesus—in fact, he was in favor of releasing Him. He didn't see anything wrong with Jesus, but he was being influenced by a crowd that did. I recently heard a genuine word from the Lord out of this text that shook me like a leaf. He said to me, "This is the Pilate generation. Many don't find fault in Jesus, but they're being influenced by a crowd that does."

As Pilate teetered between siding with Jesus and pleasing the crowd, the Scripture records that the crowd was "insistent, demanding with loud voices that He be crucified. And the voices of these men and of the chief priests prevailed." (Luke 23:23 NKJV)

The only way to win over a Pilate generation is to be louder than the crowd. Silence loses this game every time. If the devil is insistent, you and I refuse to move. If the kingdom of darkness starts making demands, we adjourn the devil with a superior authority. If the entire kingdom of darkness lifts up its voice, the church lifts up one louder. God wants people. The devil wants people. We are in competition to obtain the precious souls of people hanging in the balance.

Pilate represents a generation of people who are able to be influenced. When the church begins to influence those who are able to influence others, we have maximized our impact. Jesus came and died to save the world. A lot of the world hasn't found out about it because a lot of the church hasn't talked about it. Jesus came to heal the world. A lot of the world doesn't believe that because a lot of the church doesn't even believe that.

A vocal church is a winning church. Let's take the mute button off of our walk with Jesus. Now is not the time to shrink back or turn down the volume. Now is the time to get louder.

Father, I want a pure display of Your love and righteousness upon my life in season and out of season. Hardship won't silence me. All of the kingdom of darkness combined won't silence me. The world won't silence me. I will be louder. In Jesus' name, amen.